DRAUGAR

The Girl with the Golden Buddha

The Seventh Scribe

PEGASUS BOOKS

Pegasus Books
8165 Valley Green Drive
Sacramento, CA 95820
www.pegasusbooks.net

First Edition: January 2019
Published in North America by Pegasus Books. For information, please contact Pegasus Books c/o Marcus McGee, 8165 Valley Green Drive, Sacramento, CA 95823.

Library of Congress Cataloguing-In-Publication Data
The Seventh Scribe
Draugar: The Girl with the Golden Buddha/The Seventh Scribe– 1st ed
p. cm.
Library of Congress Control Number: 2018959307
ISBN – 978-1-941859-76-6

1. SCIENCE / Physics / Quantum Theory. 2. TECHNOLOGY & ENGINEERING / Biomedical. 3. HEALTH & FITNESS / Longevity. 4. RELIGION / Spirituality. 5. PHILOSOPHY / Free Will & Determinism. 6. PHILOSOPHY / Metaphysics. 7. RELIGION / Biblical Commentary / Old Testament

10 9 8 7 6 5 4 3 2 1

Comments about *Draugar: The Girl with the Golden Buddha* and requests for additional copies, book club rates and author speaking appearances may be addressed to The Seventh Scribe or Pegasus Books c/ Marcus McGee, 8165 Valley Green Drive, Sacramento, CA 95823., or you can send your comments and requests via e-mail to mmcgee@pegasusbooks.net.

Also available as an eBook from Internet retailers and from Pegasus Books

Printed in the United States of America

The question of sexual dominance can exist only in the nightmare of that soul which has armed itself, totally, against the possibility of the changing motion of conquest and surrender... which is love.

James Baldwin

For my brothers

Again, sometimes we are forced to accept an existentialism that can no longer be ignored, where the lines between allegory and reality are blurred. My story is as real as your believing.

Help me!

DRAUGAR

The Girl with the Golden Buddha

What is it about the law of attraction? If males were smart, then there would be no future generations. Males—what spell overtakes us and makes us oblivious to the danger, to the sticky webs that ensnare us? What foolishness compels us to ignore our healthy fear, ignore the obvious so we are willing to contest the carefully-crafted trap?

Outmatched in all capacities, we are the sad, pathetic victims of our own compulsion-driven nature. Perhaps there is a fleeting moment at our inevitable demise when we *do* understand, when we might recognize our proper place within the dark, evolving web of destiny, but then... maybe not.

My brothers, you'd be mistaken if you've assumed I'm referencing the relationship between a human male and human female, or a relationship between any two humans for that matter. While I was never successful at them, human relationships are occasionally healthy and important, producing fine fruit, but humans are not alone in this world.

A month ago, I would have never believed it, but there are dark, ancient, perpetual, predatory creatures within our midst, and for most, they are impossible to recognize—no, not until the very end.

When I met her at a downtown coffee shop on the first day of October, I felt the instant attraction between us. She was young, glowing, beautiful and intriguing—possessing the understated wisdom of ages. Her hair was blond-ish, twisted in a braid of wispy dreadlocks, and her face, with high cheekbones and delicate features, was a seeming alabaster work of classic art. When she smiled at me, I was ensnared by the first sticky line.

What does a human male do upon encountering such a creature—that singularity, that force of nature with the potential to completely fill all the long-vacant spaces of his heart and soul? He stops in his tracks, or at the edge of chance, and he either seizes the opportunity or he lives a lifetime of regret. I never considered for once that she was at the center of a well-designed, intricate and effective web—the web of Destiny.

October 1 – First Glance

It just so happened that I found myself standing across from a beautiful female as I awaited my coffee order. I wasn't in a real relationship, but I was involved with someone who left me feeling empty and unfulfilled. Thus, with great difficulty I feigned disinterest as I stood next to the incredible female, though I was ready to do anything to ensure seeing her again.

We exchanged a smile and a "hello" at the counter, and then she took a table near a large window in the front of the coffee shop to enjoy her beverage and a vegetable sandwich. I approached, wary, though keeping my distance.

"I haven't seen you in here before. Are you new to downtown?"

"I am," she answered. "I'm here for the month. I'm sure you'll see me if you're around. I'm Sally."

"Very nice to meet you, Sally. Do you mind if I sit?"

She nodded. I sat.

"Please forgive me," I said, "I don't think we've met before today, but you seem so familiar. I'm thinking I've met you somewhere else recently. I just can't remember where."

"Maybe you've seen me in your dreams."

"No, but that's strange. I was just thinking I haven't been able to remember any of my dreams lately. It's been bothering me. What about you—do I seem familiar to you?"

"You seem... interesting to me," she laughed. "Maybe we could *become* familiar?"

"Where do you work?" I asked. "Where are you from?

"Look, I'm sorry, but I don't have time for a full-blown interview. I have to be back at the sanctuary in fifteen minutes, and I still have to eat."

I savored every second as she ate, my eyes and mind tracing her face in memory. I even remembered the very design of her delicate hands.

"You have an *European* look."

"I call myself a global mutt," she laughed, "but my family's originally from Norway."

"Norway?"

"I have a grandmother there," she answered. "My father came to the U.S. as a young man. Do you work around here?"

"I'm a writer," I admitted, embarrassed. "I have an office on the next block."

"What do you write?"

"Thrillers. What do you read?"

"I like stories that challenge belief," she said, glancing across the room. "Humans are uncomfortable embracing the unconventional. Are you?"

"I wouldn't be uncomfortable embracing anything you might like," I ventured.

God punishes cheesy lines, so I expected a divine rebuke, but not a test. My eyes followed as she pulled a plastic Ziploc bag from her purse that seemed at first to contain a slice of chocolate cake, but when she poured it onto the plate, I knew instantly what it was, though I had no idea why she had put it there. It was a hunk of moist dirt, sliced in a form that resembled a dessert portion. But maybe I was wrong.

"Is... is that really dirt?"

"It is," she smiled, "but not just any dirt. I ordered it online. It's actually very healthy." She scooped a morsel onto a plastic fork and filled her mouth, relishing as she swallowed. "Delicious! Wanna try a bite? I'll understand if you don't want to."

"Of course I'll try it," I insisted before I seriously considered my answer. If it would impress her enough to see me again, it was worth a try.

I nodded, motioning for her to share, and she forked a large portion and placed it in my open mouth. *Okay, it tasted like dirt!* I gagged at the thought of swallowing it, regretting that I had so rashly taken a mouthful of soil for consumption. I had tasted dirt as a child, but I had never eaten it. I had read that, in many countries, certain women have a propensity to eat dirt. They're called *geophagi*, or Earth-eaters. Unconventional? *Challenging belief?*

I was determined to see Sally again, so if that meant embracing new experiences, I was on-board. Straining, I swirled the mud sludge, creating more saliva, and swallowed the thick ooze.

"Different," I concluded, swigging my coffee to rinse the soil and grit from my teeth, "but not as bad as I thought. How often do you... eat the... earth?"

"Every day," she answered, standing. "Keeps me connected. You're sweet—I respect you for being brave enough to try it. Maybe we will be familiar after all."

"Will you be here around the same time tomorrow?" I asked.

"Maybe," she flirted. "Aren't you afraid I might share another dessert?"

"I'll be here. I hope to see you again."

"Don't worry," she smiled, gently stroking my cheek. "You will... and you're a writer, so bring a book."

An hour later, after her spell had broken, I couldn't believe what I had done, though my mind was on fire. There was something about Sally—something beyond the experience, beyond the physical—that captured my focus and stirred my soul.

Yet there was the innate fight-or-flight warning mechanism stirring within me that said, *"Run, now!"*—a spleen-inspired caution that challenged vanity, curiosity and lust. And yet like the guileless male spider, I stepped across the first sticky line and moved toward the powerful presence at the center of the web.

October 2 – Sally

Sally Shippman. When I arrived at 1:45 the next day, she told me her full name. She was wearing black faux suede boots with fitted black denim pants and a top that clung to her narrow waist, tracing firm, natural breasts. She wore little make up, which would have been an affront to nature's grace. And whereas I'd spent the day practicing what I would say to her, my supple silver tongue became lead.

"It's nice to see you again" she said, perky. "Having a good day?"

"Getting better. I, uh… I researched Earth-eating last night. I even ordered a sample."

"Are you always so quickly familiar with women you randomly meet at coffee shops?"

"I've never met anyone like you before," I assured her. "I'd like to know you better."

"Well," she sighed, coquettish, "you really don't want to know me better. I'm giving you a head start. Run now, while you have the chance. You deserve to be happy."

"I should be afraid of you?" I asked. "I thought you might be put-off by me being so direct."

"No, I like you, and that's why you should get out now. You should get up from this table, turn away from me and never look back. Scurry away, little boy. Forget about me. That's my advice."

"And miss out on getting to know you? What would I have to fear from you?"

"I'm a force of nature," she cautioned. "In the end, nature is efficient and does what it must. Hey, I'm just being authentic."

"This is different. You're different," I said, confused. "I feel something between us. Would you really want me to just walk away and never look back?"

"It's not important what I want or think," she maintained. "I feel something between us, too. That's why I'm telling you that you should run now… to save your life, while you're still capable."

"You don't understand. I've been *looking* for you my entire life. You're everything I have ever wanted. Why would I walk away or run when I've finally met you?"

"I won't tell you what to do," she said with a smile, "but don't ever say I didn't warn you."

My heart fluttered as she reached over with a beautiful, manicured hand, stroking my cheek. I peered into her soft, penetrating eyes. She was the match of an angel, a goddess, and apparently, she had a dark sense of humor.

"Why should I worry?" I asked. "Are you a crazy ax-murderer? A serial killer?"

"No, I'm something much worse."

I still remember the expression on her face when she said those words, "something much worse." I remember thinking she was the sexiest woman I had ever met. I didn't know why, but the warning really turned me on. *Run for my life?* More like run *with* it.

"What time are you off work, Sally?" I asked. "Can I take you out to dinner?"

"I'm sorry, but I'm busy until late tonight, and I have to be up in the morning."

"Then can I have your phone number. Maybe we could talk later?"

"Of course we can talk later," she answered, "but I won't be up for a phone call tonight. Will you be here tomorrow?"

"I'll be here."

"Then we'll talk tomorrow," she said, reaching over and squeezing my hand. "I'll look forward to it."

"Not as much as I will," I called as she rose and headed for the door.

My eyes fell to her waist, hips and shapely butt as she walked into the distance. I took a deep breath. Her presence left electric traces in the air, a sort of sensual ionization that lingered long after she was gone. I was compelled to follow, as if in a trance over the next few minutes. When I knew anything, I was standing in front of a building three blocks away.

October 3 – Mystery Man

By one o'clock that afternoon, I felt a tinge of anxiety. Why didn't I simply insist on getting Sally's phone number? *Because it seemed like she didn't want to give it to me.* Maybe I was being paranoid, but I had asked her directly for it, and she deflected. And that business about walking away and forgetting her—it was cute, but I hoped she'd stop with the creepy warnings.

Maybe I came off as inappropriate or too aggressive, but Mel always insisted that *fortune favors the bold.* Then again, we live in a time of sensitivity about sexual harassment. I must have come on too strong! It's why she didn't give me her number!

Maybe she wasn't interested, or *she* decided to turn and run in another direction. It was already 1:35. She had been at the table near the window by 1:15 on the previous two days.

"I'm sorry I'm here a little later today," she said as she sat with her beverage at 1:45. "How's your day?"

"It's been a good day," I answered. "I had a little time, so I did some research on your family name. 'Shippman, or Schippmann' from Norway, and it comes from the Old Norse, meaning 'ship maker.' Your ancestors must have built boats. Maybe you come from Vikings. Is that what you were warning me about?"

"There are things in Norway scarier than Vikings," she answered. "Maybe you better do a little more research. You'll see."

"Before I forget," I interrupted, "I wanted to check if you were coming this afternoon, but I don't have your phone number."

"Oh, I'm sorry. It's 916-372-8427. I'll put it in your phone if you'd like." I passed her my phone and watched as she dialed the numbers, took a selfie and created a profile. "Just call me this afternoon so I'll have yours. What time is it?"

"Two o'clock. Why?"

"He's meeting me here. I have to give him a key to my condo." She glanced toward the door, her eyes meeting those of a muscular, handsome man who entered. He smiled as he started toward the table. "I really want you to meet him," she said.

Who? I thought, heartbroken. *Your boyfriend? Why would I want to meet him?* I should have known. Women like Sally didn't go long unclaimed. I instantly resented him and watched jealously as he kissed her once on each cheek. Sensing my discomfort, she took my hand, seeming to claim me.

"This is the guy I told you about," she said to the man, who nodded toward me, reaching out. I shook his hand reluctantly.

"It is a real pleasure to meet you," he said. "I'm Erick Draugar. My daughter here seems to be quite taken with you of late. As a father, I could ask you to look after her, but she's very capable of taking care of herself... and of you too."

"Father?" I said, incredulous. *The man looked as young or younger than I did!* I figured Sally had to be in her late twenties at best, so her father would have to be at least fifty, but he literally looked as young as she did—more like a brother... or a boyfriend. "Okay, so you're really Sally's father?"

"Wait—you are thinking I am her boyfriend?" he laughed, a Nordic-Saxon accent flavoring his voice. "I'm sorry. We get that all the time, don't we, Sally? People tell me I look young for my age. We've got good genes, I guess."

"Unbelievable genes," I remarked, observing the eye contact between the two. "If someone told me you were thirty, I'd believe it. Is this some kinda joke?"

"He's being silly," Sally said to her father as she shot me a disapproving glare. "I'm proud to have a father who looks so young and handsome. Let's all sit."

"I'm sorry," I sighed. "It's just that I think Sally's really special."

"We have that in common," he smiled, winking at her.

"Just wondering..." I asked, clearing my throat, scheming. "Do you remember who won the 1970 World Series?"

"Of course I do!" he laughed. "In 1970, it was the Baltimore Oriels and the Cincinnati Reds. Baltimore won the series four to one, with Palmer, McNally and Cuellar pitching."

He was right, which meant his memory had to be at least in its fifties, I determined.

"You like American sports?" he asked. "Then you must remember when the Dallas Cowboys joined the football league, which was the same year Rozelle from the Rams became commissioner. It was... the Eagles and the Packers in the championship game that year—in December. Philadelphia won. Should I go on?"

I nodded my head, but I didn't remember back that far. Okay, he knew about sports, but he could have looked up that stuff.

"My daughter tells me you're a writer?" he asked. "And you write thrillers?"

"Thrillers and a few other things. I just started on a film project."

"You like dark themes and tragedy, I understand? Well, believe it or not, Truman Capote was a friend of mine. In fact, I was in Kansas with Truman and Harper Lee right after the Clutter family murders. I stayed through the interviews. Really dark stuff there. Long time ago..."

"Don't worry, Dad," Sally said, interrupting his nostalgic moment, "you'll always be a young man as far as I'm concerned."

Maybe I was being pranked? After taking a second look at him, I thought I was able to detect what seemed to be a gray hair near his left temple—one accidently left out of the *Just for Men* regimen. Otherwise, his hair and short beard were uniformly brown. He plainly didn't look a day over thirty! Maybe it *was* in the blood—good genes.

"I don't use *Just for Men*," he said, seeming to read my mind. "I've never heard of it."

"How did you know what I was thinking?" I asked.

"Oh well, kids," he said, ignoring my question as he stood. "Duty calls. I gotta go." He kissed Sally again before turning to me. "You—I read all your books last night."

"All of them? That's impossible."

"I'm a voracious reader, especially when I have an interest. I told Sally this morning that I wanted to meet you, and just so you know, I officially approve. You'll do."

*****

She was gathering her things to leave by the time he left, but I had to go through with my plan.

"Sally, I was thinking I'd like to take you out for dinner tomorrow night—wherever you want to go. Your father just said he approved. What kind of food do you like?"

"I'm vegan," she answered. "Is that a problem for you?"

"No, not at all. I like vegans... and vegetables—as long as they're humanely-treated. How long have you been one of those?"

"For more years than I can remember—for lifetimes. I think the breeding and killing of animals for human consumption is wrong on so many levels."

"Vegetables, coffee and dirt? That's what you eat?"

"I don't eat animals or animal products, but I might eat you."

"Well, I'm excited! I'll find a vegan restaurant. Dinner tomorrow night?"

"Well, I guess so, since you've met my father and he likes you. Last chance to cut and run!"

"No, I want to pursue this."

"Okay, then it's dinner, tomorrow night. Later is better. Find a place that's open after ten."

October 4 – First Date

When I arrived at her condo at nine-thirty to pick her up, a three-legged torti cat met me outside the door. It mewed and slinked to a place between my ankles. Her condo was in an old neighborhood with huge oak trees, American elms, towering pines and historic homes that created dark shadows.

To the left of the door was a basket of tan, orange and purple gourds, which was next to a place mat that displayed the word, "*Háski*[1]." To the right of the door sat an eighteen-inch-tall, mud-encrusted, seated sculpture of buddha, ascetic though auspicious. I knocked.

"You're late, but I'm not ready yet," Sally said after opening the door. "Come in. Help yourself to a glass of wine. I won't be long."

I could hardly believe my eyes as I examined the Bordeaux wine bottle with the words "*1787 LaFite*" and "*Th. J*" crudely drawn in white paint strokes. The dark bottle looked ancient and dusty, but I fancied it a souvenir she kept and refilled... until I swirled the brownish liquid, the aroma wafting to my nose. It was an earthy wine, with hints of cedar, cassis, spice, tobacco, truffle, and dark red berries. It was pure ambrosia on my palate. *An incredible counterfeit!*

Looking around the space, I got the distinct impression that she was into fine art. There was a large, colorful, swirling,

---

1 Old Icelandic –"*peril*" or "*danger*"

haunting oil painting of a mother and child hanging on the main wall, and to the right of it, an unassuming mahogany table (18th century George III Sideboard, *after an Internet search*).

There were a few items on the table surface, which included a medieval dagger with a crude steel ten-inch blade and ivory hilt (there was a residue on the blade, which to me seemed to be dried blood). There was also a hangman's noose, braided from red silk, a Colt .45-caliber revolver that seemed to come directly from the Old West, six silver bullets and a jar of colorful stones that had the appearance of semi-precious gems. *A little odd*, I thought, *but well within the range of acceptance for a dark mind.*

On one wall, I saw a painting that I recognized: *The Storm on the Sea of Galilee* by Rembrandt from 1633. I'm not an expert, but the painting had a sense of authenticity that begged attention, so I took a closer look. I'd heard that it'd been stolen in the 1990s. And on another wall, I recognized the priceless *Chez Tortoni* by Manet. And books—her bookshelf held a tome containing a worn and ancient notebook attributed to Leonardo—the rudimentary sketches and commentary of da Vinci in pen and ink. *Impossible!* I thought.

"I see you've met Mama," Sally said as she came down the stairs and spotted the cat next to me on the sofa.

"Mama?"

"I think she likes you. That's a good sign. Mama's got good instincts about humans. I'm ready to go."

*****

She was beautiful in a black dress and heels, the dark fabric contrasting remarkably with her sun-starved skin. Her dreadlocks rested on bare supple shoulders, and the outfit snugly embraced womanly features—a contoured waist and luscious hips above shapely legs, ankles and feet. I had to take a deep breath to restore the oxygen lost to my brain. I had never seen a woman more appealing at first glance.

"You look... very nice."

She walked toward me and kissed me directly on the mouth, nipping my lower lip hard enough to elicit blood. I cringed as we hugged.

"You look good... enough to eat," she said, smiling. "I'm starved. Are you gonna feed me?"

*****

In her eyes, as I looked across the restaurant table into cold pale-blue eyes—I was sure I saw a reflection of my own soul, but hers were hungry eyes. We had gone to a vegan cafe in midtown that ranked "most-popular" in the city on *Yelp*, though I wished we had gone to a less-populated place.

Despite my 9:45 reservation, we did not get seated until 10:30, and by that time, it seemed the kitchen had all but sold out of its most popular items. Rather than sitting across the table, I sat next to her, our fingers interlinked in her lap.

"I want asparagus tonight, and wild mushrooms—oh, and something with taro root. The cilantro pesto here is excellent, and so is the eggplant. I absolutely love eggplant!"

Fifteen minutes later, we were eating a savory roasted red bell pepper-and-heirloom tomato soup, and crunchy vegan quinoa spinach bites with a gingered, orange-honey dipping sauce. Our sweating wineglasses were one-third filled with a four-year-old decanted Napa Fume Blanc, presenting soft, rich tropical fruit—guava and mango, with hints of citrus—leading to a mouthwatering finish.

"I want to know more about you," I said, "but because I don't want tonight to sound like an interview, I thought I'd limit myself to three questions..."

"Three questions? Interesting," she laughed, "but before you ask them, I have one condition."

"Which is?"

"Before each question, tell me why you chose that particular question, and not another."

"Okay," I nodded, "that's fair. First question: *What does Sally want?* I chose that question because it answers the more central question, *'Why?'* Why are you here? Why aren't you married? Why do you get out of bed in the morning?"

"Oh, that's easy," she answered. "I want *to know.* The only thing I'm sure of is that I'm here for a reason—so my life's purpose is *to know* the reason, wherever that leads me. It's why *we're* here."

"We? Tonight? At this restaurant? *This* was supposed to happen, between you and me?"

"It sure did," she nodded, smiling. "For years, I've been seeking an echo, a vibration at the right frequency—a compatible counter-point. When I call out to the universe, it's what comes back to me, my perfect complement. What's your next question?"

"My next question: *What do you believe?* and I ask that question because I'm convinced that we construct unique interfaces to the world and to others, which are based on what we believe is true, or real. We create our own laws of gravity, order and morality. So that question also answers the question, *Who are you?* since our beliefs *are* the interface. Do you believe in divinity? Balance? Good and evil?"

"That's a more difficult question," she answered, sipping the wine, "because I believe in all things and I believe in nothing at the same time. This existence—it's completely real, while none of it is real. It matters, and it doesn't matter. I actually believe that you and I are in for an adventure ahead," she laughed, "but I think you should have asked the more appropriate question, *'Do* you believe?' to which I would have answered, *Yes.* Third question, and then we order dinner. I'm famished."

"*What do you fear and regret?* which answers, *What motivates you? What are you willing to wager, based on the first two questions?* Take 'love,' for example, which is a gamble and always in peril. Fear is the limiting factor in human experience as it relates to the first question, and risk is central to the second question. So what are you willing to risk, based on what you believe? Risk of loss informs fear, which goes right back to personal motivation."

"I fear and regret perpetual existence—immortality. At some point, it all has to end. There must be a conclusion, a period at the end of the sentence, the last page of the book... the actual answer to your first question, *Why?* I fear that I'm a creature of the night, and one who'll never die, is cursed to roam the Earth to never find the answers to the questions you just asked."

I saw such profound sadness in her eyes—perhaps even agony, and at that moment, I realized my sudden descent as I fell... in love with Sally. She was dark and protective outwardly, but only to hide her self-perceived weakness, her vulnerable soul... her repressed hope.

*****

We had the vegan Shepherd's Pie under gravy for dinner, with sautéed ginger-garlicked asparagus and wild mushrooms on the side. By the time we finished our second bottle of wine, we were laughing and talking like old friends.

"I brought us a special treat!" she piped, beaming.

"What is it?"

"Dessert, all the way from Norway." She asked the server for two small plates and removed a tin container from her purse. "You seemed to enjoy it before. It's from a bog!"

Great! more dirt—this time shaped in the form of a slice of chocolate cake, but it was still dirt, sludge or mud. If I hadn't been semi-intoxicated, I may have declined, but the night was going so well, and who knew where it would lead?

"Bring it on."

I had difficulty with the last few bites because the wine was gone. I ordered a coffee to wash the last few clods down. Arm around her waist, we walked a few blocks in the city to settle our dinners and dirt, and then I drove her home.

She stopped at the front door, where Mama appeared to be blocking my advance. Glancing down, I recognized Sally would not invite me in.

"Thank you," she whispered, hugging me. "I had a great time tonight. It was fun."

I wrapped my arms around her firm body, pulling her close, feeling her warmth against me, and then she kissed me—a real kiss—with soft lips, an open mouth and a deep sigh.

"It was a beautiful night," I whispered. "We'll have to do it again."

"What are you doing tomorrow night?" she asked. "I'd like to take *you* somewhere. My treat!"

October 5 – The Moth and the Flame

She asked me to pick her up at 11 p.m., and she was standing outside her door when I pulled up to the curb at 11:10. The autumn nights were becoming nippy, so she wore brown calf-high boots, factory-torn jeans and a light denim jacket with a low-cut, flimsy silk top. I wore black slacks and dress shoes with a pull-over black sweater. She approached the car and got in.

"Where are we headed?" I asked.

"You'll see when we get there."

She directed me to a place in mid-town, a place I must have driven past hundreds of times without ever noticing it was there. Inside, the Middle-Eastern-themed lounge bustled on that Friday night, reeking of strong Turkish coffee and the sweet aroma of flavored tobacco. On the counter were an assortment of devices that looked like shiny, colorful genie lamps with hoses and small bowls at their tops.

"You ever have hookah?" she asked.

"No."

"Our first adventure!"

At the counter, she ordered a two-hose hookah with a perforated aluminum foil-wrapped bowl, packed with flavored tobacco (or *Mu'assel*) and two pints of locally-brewed craft beers. A man seated us outside at a small wooden table under an awning, where a few other couples were already seated and smoking. There was a large flickering candle in the center of the table.

Minutes later, a server came over to the table and placed three one-inch charcoal cubes on the aluminum screen over the tobacco, which began to smoke. After sipping her dark beer, Sally took up the hose and drew a deep breath, blowing out a cloud.

"Your turn."

I had never puffed a cigarette, so I wasn't certain I'd be able to inhale the smoke, but I was pleasantly surprised as it filled my lungs—it was cool and mild. I blew out blissfully and repeated the experience.

"Nice, Sally!"

Her eyes were distracted by a small fluttering insect that flitted about the candle flame.

"I could save him, but it'll do him no good. He'll just find another flame. He can't help himself."

"There's another one," I noted. "And another. Wow! I never noticed."

"Men are moths," she sighed. "It's sad, in a way... watching them die."

"Men or moths?" I joked.

"I tried to save him," she answered, eyes transfixed, "but he couldn't escape himself. He died anyway."

"Who died?"

"Rai."

"Who's Rai."

"The last man I dated. He died a year ago this month?"

"What happened?" I asked. "How'd he die?"

"Like they all die," she answered. "He flew into the flame and burned away to nothing."

"What flame?"

"Mine... well, not exactly. Hers. But I'm a flame. I tried to warn both of you."

"You're putting me on," I countered, taking another puff from the hose. "That sounds bizarre. Rai was your boyfriend? Is he really dead? How did he die?"

"Class IV Hemmorage, but that's not what killed him."

"A Class IV Hemmorage is serious. What killed him then? There had to be a cause on a death certificate."

"Medical examiners always get it wrong. 'Capitulation' *is* a major cause of death, no matter what a death certificate might say."

"What does it have to do with moths, which are irrelevant to anything important to tonight?"

"Their very nature makes them helpless prey. There is a bioluminescent worm within a cave in Waitomo, New Zealand. It's called a "glowing spider-worm," and she recreates the sky above the Earth, deceiving males of many species, especially the moths, to fly into the web of sticky traps. They mimic in the night available, receptive females to ensnare the hormone-driven males. How is it any different for any other males? The male is weak beyond imagining. Oh, I don't want to talk about it anymore!"

Just then, a third moth crashed onto the table, legs and antenna singed, wings wilting, smoking. It was my first time imagining what an insect was feeling. It was a personal male tragedy on a miniature scale. Not one to let a few dead moths ruin the night, I tried to change the subject, but I had already lost her. She seemed desolate, inconsolable.

"I really like you," she said, her voice trailing, her face dour. "There's destiny between us, but I've already read the story. Things will never work out for us. Please take me home now."

October 6 – The Woman and the Crab

I went to the coffee shop at one o'clock and waited there until four, but she never came in that day. I was losing her. *What had I done wrong?* I replayed our conversation from the hookah lounge over and over again in my mind. How did we get on the subject of her ex-boyfriend anyway? Was she still in love with him? Was he really dead, or had she engaged in hyperbole? Was it just a break-up? She seemed profoundly devastated by the loss.

I called at seven o'clock that evening and got her answering machine.

"Hi Sally. It's me. Missed you at the coffee shop today. Hey, are you okay? You seemed a little sad last night. Call me if you want to talk."

A little after eight, I felt the urge to call her again, but I didn't want to seem anxious, so I decided I'd wait until nine-thirty. It was Saturday. Maybe she worked later shifts on weekends. Surely she would be home by nine-thirty.

This is Sally. I am not able to answer the phone right now. Please leave a message and I'll get back to you. Beep.

I didn't leave a second message because I had already said what I wanted to say... but I didn't want to simply hang up. I did end the call, however, after ten seconds of vacillation. She had to know I was calling. I wouldn't call back.

I started worrying at 11:30. What if something happened to her? What if the depression I witnessed on the hookah bar patio had become too much? What if she had gone inside and overdosed or slit her wrists? That would explain why she wasn't at the coffee shop and why she wasn't answering my calls.

Two nights before, she said "it all had to end." Reluctant, I got in the car and drove past her condo, guilty, feeling like a stalker. I saw lights on in her living room and kitchen and heard a Nina Simone song playing through an open window. Maybe she'd been out on a date and had company over? I didn't dare stop.

I got home at 11:50, feeling depressed that, while I had seen her every day since we met—for five straight days—I wouldn't even get a chance to talk to her on the sixth. To my surprise, my phone rang at 11:59.

"I'm reading one of your books."

"Which one?" I asked, relieved.

"The story about the human female and the crab—*The Crab Story*[2]. I have a question."

"About the story? What is it?"

"Was she a human female or a force of nature?" she asked. "The crab must have known the relationship would never work out."

---

[2] From *Synchronicity*, published in 2001

"He thought love would overcome all, would transform him into something more than what he was."

"Maybe he was *already* more than he thought he was?" she offered. "Maybe he just thought he was a crab when he was actually something else."

"I don't think so. How could he not know what he was?"

"And when he realized their being together was impossible?"

"It was too late," I answered. "Love transformed him into a fool... the way it transforms most men."

"And only then he realized what *she* was," she concluded, "*a force of nature that devoured him*. Tell me, where did that story come from?"

"From my Muse, from Melpomene. I hardly remember writing it."

"Then it's a warning," Sally said. "You should listen to her."

"That's not my interpretation of the story," I countered. "At the time I wrote it, I was engaged to a woman who was like a vampire—she took and took and would have kept taking until there was nothing left. If the story was a warning, then it spared me from that woman and saved my soul. It doesn't apply to you."

"Why have you chosen me of all females you could have chosen?" she asked. "You're an attractive, successful man who should have no problem getting women. I figured you'd have moved on already."

"I don't want just any woman, Sally. I want a force of nature, but the *right* force of nature. I want you."

"You didn't learn anything from *the foolish little crab* you wrote about? And you didn't watch the pitiful moths crashing and burning last night? You didn't see the warning?"

"Warning? Maybe it's destiny," I answered. "You tell me, what happens to the moths that *don't* fly into the flame?"

"They probably find females, get laid and then they die happy... or they don't, cuz they've got no balls."

"Moth balls—" I laughed, "Very funny. So which is better," I asked, "a mere moment of pleasure (if it's even good for moths), or going out in a blaze of glory?"

"Depends on which moth you ask," she giggled. "You're persistent, if nothing else. I volunteer early in the morning, so I've gotta get some sleep."

"Will you be at the coffee shop at the regular time? I didn't get to see you today."

"I don't know. We'll see. Goodnight."

October 7 – The Mama Cat Paradox

On Sunday afternoon, I waited at the coffee shop for five hours, hoping. Thinking ahead, I brought my laptop so that I could work while I was there. Sally never showed. The three calls I made went directly to voicemail. Sitting there, I reflected on our last conversation. I was finally starting to believe she really didn't want me to pursue her, or she had committed me to "just friends" status. *Damn male moths!*

Maybe she had found another boyfriend. I started writing a new story that afternoon, hoping Melpomene would provide distraction from my recent obsession. Mel was always there for me, especially in the dark hours.

As I yielded, Mel whispered an intriguing plot about a dangerous creature in the guise of a woman into my right ear/left brain, but Mel had always been jealous of my love interests. She often went out of her way to sabotage budding or promising relationships. Based on our history, Mel probably despised Sally and saw her as a treacherous rival.

I was at home broiling a fresh, wild sockeye salmon filet when the phone rang.

"Wanna come over?"

*****

I brought two bottles of wine, a two-year-old Semillon from Sonoma, described as *a full-bodied ripe white, blended with 17% Sauvignon Blanc. A gravelly texture and mineral undertone curb its peach and fig flavors...* and a 2014 bottle of Mynster, a dessert wine from Sjaellands Odde in Denmark, but only because I couldn't find a Nordic after-dinner wine.

"Are you hungry? I made pasta with fresh heirloom tomatoes, basil and oregano. I waited for you. Everything's still warm."

Midway through dinner, wine bottle two-thirds gone, I grew bold enough to reach over and squeeze her hand.

"I thought I'd never see you again. Why did you decide to invite me over?"

"I had a bad dream," she sighed, "and I woke up, feeling sad and lonely. Then I thought of you."

"I live alone too. I know how you feel."

"But I don't live alone," she countered. "Mama lives here. She's just a little withdrawn lately. She's getting old."

"How long have you had her?"

"I don't 'have' her, goofy. We live together," she answered. "She's Mama."

It made no sense, but it wasn't worth an argument. I wasn't exactly alone either. I had Mel, but no one would understand our relationship.

"Is Mama a vegan too?"

"Don't be silly. She eats meat, mostly fish and chicken."

"Isn't that a bit of a paradox?" I asked. "A vegan who lives with a meat-eating animal? You told me you were a vegan because you didn't believe in the breeding and exploitation of animals for purposes of consumption."

"Human consumption," she clarified. "It's natural for animals to eat animals. Circle of life? Karma? Animals eat other animals, but they don't exploit the females. The flesh industry is the cruel and senseless exploitation of femalekind."

"Where's the difference?" I asked. "Aren't humans animals too? So every time you take a case of cans or a sack of cat food off the shelf to buy it, the market will replace those items, right? which means the fish and chicken Mama eats will have to be bred and exploited, which means the females. If humans shut down all the farms, the millions of dogs and cats on the planet would starve to death, right? Mama would starve."

"I'm not asking for farms to be shut down. I just refuse to be a part of the unacceptable mistreatment of females on the Earth... for human purposes."

Probably not the best conversation for getting on her good side, but I rarely passed up the opportunity for a spirited debate. I uncorked the Mynster (which to me looked like "Monster"), hoping to change the subject.

"Have you ever been back to Norway, Sally?"

"I've gone a few times with my dad over the years. We have relatives there, and property."

"Did you enjoy your time there?"

"I explored my history," she answered. "I discovered there what I am."

"Any Viking ancestors?"

After bowing her head for a moment in contemplation, she leaned then toward me and kissed me.

"You're a worldly man. Have you ever heard the term: *draugr*?"

"Draugr? No. What is that?"

"Draugar have the ability to enter dreams. Have you ever been visited in the night?"

Melpomene visited me in trances on occasion, and a few times in bed, taking the form of a mischievous Moroccan or Egyptian temptress, but I was loath to share that secret.

"I've had nightmares."

"I don't mean nightmares," she differed. "After you go home and fall asleep tonight, you'll dream, and I'll come to you. I'll be there."

"You'll be in my *dream*? How could you do that?"

"If I come to you tonight, will you run away?"

"I'd never run from you," I insisted.

"It'll be your last chance," she warned. "Remember your vain little crab. After tonight, it'll be too late."

October 8 – The Gift

For the first hour after I awoke on Monday morning at six, I had no recollection of even dreaming, not until I unlocked my phone and heard the Ella Fitzgerald song I had on when I fell asleep—*I'll See You in My Dreams*. Returning the phone to the nightstand, I sat back and remembered.

I was walking along in a snowy pastoral scene with white-capped mountains to the left and a dense, foreboding forest to the right. The foggy morning air was cold enough to erupt in blossoming billows each time I exhaled a breath.

The landscape beneath my fur-covered boots was uneven, alternating between tall grass, slushy marsh and large, unsteady icy rocks. I could see the smoking chimney from a cottage in the distance at the edge of the tree line. Perhaps I lived there?

After walking for seeming hours toward the cottage, it did not seem to get any closer, but there was no other recognizable shelter from the worsening weather, so I soldiered on for another few hours, when to my disappointment, the cottage only seemed to be moving farther away.

Finally, I relented, reasoning I could retrace my path and return to my starting place by the way I came—when to my surprise, I suddenly found myself a few steps from the cottage door, foxfire glowing along the door frame.

Inside, I removed my reindeer fur coat and boots and stretched out on an oversized wood-carved bed before a fireplace that was ten feet tall and fifteen feet wide. A massive log, the size of a tree trunk, was ablaze, completely filling the hearth, heating the room to summertime temperatures.

Just beyond the fingertips of my right hand rested a goblet of Akvavit[3], a spirit distilled from potatoes. I had just taken a fiery mouthful when I realized I was not alone.

There was a female standing next to the bed, wrapped in a wool quilt. I didn't know her name, yet I knew who she was. She spoke a language that was foreign to me, but somehow, I understood her every word.

There was something familiar about her—her face, her eyes, her smile... and a runic ring on her finger. She let the quilt fall, exposing her graceful nude body, before climbing under the thick fur blanket and snuggling next to me.

Instantly, our naked bodies, as if created to fit together, fell into a complementary juxtaposition and we drifted off to sleep.

---

[3] Latin, meaning *water of life*

Sitting up in the bed, I suddenly remembered the dream, which seemed more real than any I had dreamed before that day. I could still feel the heat from the fireplace, hear and smell the crackling fire. And then it hit me! The female in the dream—I was unable to recognize her, but it was Sally. How could I not have known that when I was in the cottage? She had told me hours earlier that she would visit me in a dream that night.

Anxious to question her, I reached toward the phone, when to my surprise I saw the runic ring on the nightstand—the exact same ring that had been on the finger of the female in the dream. But how was that possible? Gripping it in my palm, I tested the ring's tangibility, tossing it up a few inches to gauge its weight.

It was real all right, but how had it gone from the finger of a female in a dream to a nightstand in the real world? I called Sally's phone, but she didn't answer, and I didn't have the psychological wherewithal that morning to leave a cogent message.

*****

I arrived at the coffee shop at noon and waited there until she arrived a 1:15. She placed her food and steaming drink on the table and sat across from me.

"How'd you sleep?"

"You were there!" I gasped. "You were the woman in my dream! How'd you do that?"

"How do you know the female in your dream was me?"

"Isn't *this* the runic ring I've seen you wearing on your left ring finger?" I asked while showing it in my open hand. "I can still see the indentation from where you had it on yesterday!"

"Wow! And just how would you explain that?" she asked, a little smug.

"Me?" I exclaimed. "How do *you* explain it? How is it possible for you to visit me in a dream and leave proof on my nightstand?"

"You're a writer. You research everything," she nodded. "Did you ever take the time to find out about the draugr? Did you ever look it up?"

"I can look it up now."

"No. Wait until you get home, when you're alone. It'll take some time and reflection to really understand and accept what you've gotten yourself into, and what you're going to do about it."

Taking her hand, I held the runic ring next to her finger to determine if it perfectly matched the indentation. Sally looked into my eyes, smiling, as I took her left hand in mine and slipped the ring onto her finger in a seeming public nuptial gesture.

"There! Now it's official," she nodded. "Want some dirt?"

October 9 – Draugr

I had to chair a publishing event at the local university on the previous night, and a group of us went out to a bar after the event. Friends forced me to take a Lyft home, so I was in no shape to research without sleep. I assume I had a dream or two during the restless night, but I did not remember a visitor, and there was no object left on the nightstand. I entered my home office at six a.m. and returned to my Internet research.

Draugr – also called aptrganga or aptragangr, literally "again-walker," is an undead creature from Norse mythology.

Very funny, Sally. And to think I made two attempts to ditch the lecture event to spend time researching the cryptic name she had gone out of her way to mention two days in a row!

According to the search, *draugar* were mythological creatures, meaning they weren't real. Apparently, they were the Scandinavian incarnation of the eastern European *vampire* or *zombie*, with a mindless male Viking flair, as described in Nordic folk tales, literature and video games.

Sally hinted she had a dark side. Maybe she had introduced the creature as part of an elaborate scheme to discourage me from further pursuing her. For the first time since I met her, I seriously considered her warning to run. After reading another paragraph and examining a draugr image, I was spooked enough to entertain second-thoughts about going into the coffee shop to meet her that afternoon.

However, several nagging questions lingered. How had she tricked me into dreaming about her? Perhaps she had mastered some proven "power of suggestion" technique or used hypnosis to breach the threshold of my sub-conscious mind to alter my dream state.

It wasn't impossible, since my obsession with her had predisposed such a dream. Then again, I did not recognize the female so intimately close to me in that bed as Sally. It could have been Mel. When I awoke, I probably *wanted* it to be Sally, and that's how I chose to remember things.

Draugar have the ability to enter into the dreams of the living, but it generally happens even so that they leave bedside the living person some gift, by which on awakening, the living person may be assured of the tangible nature of the visit.

Too coincidental... so what about the ring? How had she managed to place it on my nightstand as I slept? I could only conclude that she had devised some way to copy my house key and later tipped into my bedroom in the middle of the night to plant the ring.

I'm a heavy sleeper, so after a couple snifters of brandy before bed, I wouldn't have been aware of her presence. That would explain what she meant when she said she would visit me in a dream—that she would visit me when I was sleeping to whisper hypnotic words. I was impressed that Sally would have gone through so much trouble.

At that point, I believed I knew why she was so insistent about me researching draugr. She must have known there were limited Internet references, meaning I would end up at that exact site, reading those exact words. It's why she insisted she would enter my dream, and that's why she placed the ring on the nightstand.

These beings also reeked of decay and corruption. But the scariest thing about the draugr is that they had immeasurable strength and the ability to increase the size of their body at will. In some stories, they would triple their size, possibly due to drinking blood.

Reeked of decay and corruption? Hardly! On those occasions that I was at close quarters with Sally, I remember a clean, subtly spicy fragrance emanating from soft, fresh skin. After dinner on Sunday night, I had rubbed her tired back and shoulders, adoring the supple flesh that yielded to my hands and fingers. If the creatures actually were oozing, rotting corpses of the walking dead, Sally had missed that little paragraph, which made it impossible for her to be a draugr.

The resting place of the draugr was a tomb, which served much as a workable home for the creature. Draugar are able to leave this dwelling place and visit the living during the night. Such visits are supposed to be universally horrible events that often end in death for one or more of the living...

When has 'tomb' meant fancy condo? And a sexy naked female in bed with me was hardly a horrible event. I had read enough. Even if predatory, non-human females were real, like my mother sometimes had told me, Sally definitely wasn't one of them—by the very definition of 'draugr.' I never believed it for a second, but why was Sally playing such a bizarre game with me?

First, the draugr must be overcome by grappling hand-to-hand with the creature, and wrestling with it until it was subdued (Simpson, Icelandic Folktales and Legends, p. 107). The hero next must decapitate the ghost, often with a sword found in the draugr's own barrow (Chadwick, "Norse Ghosts," p. 55).

She said earlier that she liked adventure and fantasy, so perhaps she was toying with me to test my resolve. If I didn't run, then I passed the initial test, and we could start a more serious relationship. It made sense, right down to that symbolic ring ceremony on the previous afternoon! She set the whole thing up.

*****

I was surprised when I got to the coffee shop at 1:00 to find Sally already seated at our regular table, waiting for me. She stood as I approached and kissed me gently, stroking my face with soft, sculptured hands.

"Thought I'd surprise you by being here early."

"It's a pleasant surprise," I responded, bemused. "To what do I owe such a warm reception?"

"I'm happy today because of you," she said. "I think we should take the rest of the afternoon off. I feel like a nice relaxing drive down the coast."

We stopped at a local farmer's market and got fresh fruit and vegetable items for a late afternoon picnic on the beach, and we were on the road by 1:30. While driving, we discussed food, wine, politics, personal views and beliefs, with never a lull in the dialogue. Before we thought to check the clock, it was after 4:00 and we had parked.

Grabbing blankets, the food and a wine tote, we found a suitable picnic spot on the sand, left our things and took a barefoot stroll down the beach, holding hands. Pant legs rolled up, we walked at the edge of the surf, occasionally surprised by breakers that surmounted our knees.

By the time we finished eating, the sun had just begun to set, glowing bright orange as it edged closer toward the watery horizon.

"I researched draugar," I volunteered. "I had never heard the term before, but it makes sense. They're the Scandinavian version of the zombie, or the vampire."

"So after reading what you've read, do you believe that draugar are real?" she asked, "that the 'undying' walk the Earth even today?"

"I believe they're as real as zombies and vampires," I answered, "which in my opinion are incarnations of the human mind, purposed to explain and rationalize the aberrant behavior of sociopaths and serial killers in human society."

"Then how would you explain me visiting you in your dream?" she asked.

"I had a dream, okay, and it wasn't until I was awake that the woman in it seemed familiar. I don't know how you pulled it off, but you're clever. You guessed, or you manipulated me on some subliminal level."

"What if I told you I was the female who crawled next to you in that huge warm bed?" she asked. "What if I told you I was the one who poured the Akvavit for you? I started the fire in the hearth."

"Akvavit? I asked.

"The alcohol. The spirit that consumed you," she answered.

"Oh, that. Well, in addition to researching draugar, I also investigated *you*," I admitted. "I know you're a Certified Clinical Hypnotherapist, trained at the University of San Francisco. I found that little tidbit on your online C.V. So you used some form of hypnotherapy to invade my sub-consciousness, and then you controlled my dream from there."

"And the ring?"

"The only way I can explain it—you broke into my apartment and planted it on the nightstand, so I'd find it in the morning."

"Do you really think I would break into your apartment?" she asked, seeming insulted.

"There's no other way to explain it," I sighed, "You were physically in my room last night. I felt you. I'm certain of it."

"Perhaps I was," she shrugged. "But in your research last night, did you read that the draugar have the ability to *move magically through the earth, swimming through solid stone*? I think that's what the Internet says."

"I read that," I conceded, "but I also read that the draugar can be recognized by the reeking smell of their rotting flesh." I stroked her cheek. "Looking at your face, it's flawless, without a crease or wrinkle, and your essence is sensual, womanly. Draugar were dead Norse warriors. How could you possibly be a draugr?"

"Oh, aren't you a writer?" she laughed. "Surely you realize the world has changed since all those ancient exaggerated descriptions of draugar were written. There have been incredible advances in medicine.

"Draugar no longer smell like rotting flesh, and their skin is no longer *hel-blar* or *na-foir*—death blue or pale white, thanks to the work of modern draugar doctors and researchers who isolated elements from foxfire, chemicals from luciferase to create a new enzyme that counters and minimizes the detrimental effects of everlasting life"

"Good explanation," I sighed, "but I still don't believe it."

"Do you really think modern medical science wouldn't benefit draugar? You're right about vampires. They were to draugar what *neanderthal* were to *homo sapiens*. The *nosferatu* died out because they couldn't adapt, not even to sunlight. There's not much written about draugar, and most of it is outdated—fake news, but now you know."

October 11 – Tragedy

I didn't sleep all night, not for a minute. I dropped Sally off at about nine-thirty and came back to my apartment, but I was too troubled to doze off. I liked spending the waking hours with Sally, but I didn't want her invading my dreams, if that was even possible.

I didn't believe her theories about the draugar, but she was a clever storyteller. I had tested her a few times while driving, bluffing, hoping I could get her to drop the act. Right until the moment I dropped her off, she never broke character, never conceded a point.

Lying awake in bed, I wondered why she was so interested in the subject. Maybe there was a dark religious movement she discovered, a passing trend, and perhaps her explanations were so convincing because, in her heart and mind, she was convinced those old folk tales were true.

Funny—when we were at the restaurant on our first date and I asked the second question, she answered, "I believe everything and nothing at the same time." Her response was telling. Maybe it was just the season, which would soon pass.

Melpomene was at my ear all night, urging me toward the sacred writing zone I occupied when I wrote. I sensed anger from her, but then I realized it seemed more like jealousy, which made more sense.

I had neglected Mel over the last two weeks—since that first day I met Sally, but Mel had been with me from the moment I knew I was a writer, from my first independent thought. She had chosen me, and she no doubt saw Sally as a threat.

Of the nine sisters, Melpomene was always the best match for me. Early on, I engaged in flirtations with Thalia, Erato and Calliope, but with Mel, we had developed a serious, lifelong relationship. We needed each other. Initially the Muse of Chorus for humans, Mel had always been the Muse of Tragedy. Whenever I sat to write, there she was beside me.

*****

I had invited Sally over to my apartment for breakfast at ten, so I went to the early Farmer's Market and spent most of the morning cleaning and preparing a breakfast that included a Sun-Dried Tomato, Mushroom and Spinach Tofu Quiche, the last ripe blueberries of the season and a Cava *brut* from Catalonia, Spain.

She sat across from me at the table by a large window, slanted sunbeams illuminating the fresh, long-stemmed blood-red-rose arrangement and the glinting off polished silverware.

"You went through so much trouble for me?" she asked.

"No, I eat like this every morning," I joked. "Don't you?"

Unfortunately, our unique personal chemistry was "off" that morning. She seemed irritated with me about something, and I wasn't eager to engage in another discussion about draugar. We hardly talked during breakfast as a bad spirit proliferated between us. While we had an appointment for a couples' massage at noon, neither of us felt inspired to keep it.

"Maybe we're seeing too much of each other," she suggested. "I liked you better when I didn't see you so much. And stop doting on me!"

"Our conversations used to be spontaneous and inspiring," I shot back. "Now it's all doom and gloom... and draugar."

"I think we should take a little time off from each other. I miss my alone time."

"Fine by me," I sighed. "I've got a lot of work to do."

Annoyed, we parted company without even a hug. Taking a deep breath, she turned and walked to her car, never looking back, never saying goodbye.

Mel and I worked all afternoon, until the phone rang at five-thirty.

"I'm sorry to bother you," the voice said, "but we found your number in a phone as a 'last number dialed.' Do you know the female owner of a silver Honda CR-V with alloy rims?"

"Yes!" I answered, alarmed. "Her name's Sally Shippman. Is she okay?"

"Is she your wife?"

"No."

"I'm afraid there's been an accident, and things don't look good for her."

I demanded the address and weaved through dangerous rush-hour for thirty minutes in order to reach the accident site. Two ambulances were merging back onto the highway as I arrived—one with sirens and lights blaring and the other in dark silence.

Exiting my vehicle, I approached the officer who was examining her CR-V. The front end was completely crushed, smashed in an apparent head-on collision, bloody shards of glass scattered all around.

"What happened?"

"Did you know her?" the female highway patrol officer asked. "Poor girl. She never saw it coming. Turns out—truck driver—big rig on the other side of the highway, goin in the other direction—he musta been textin or fell asleep and lost control. Came right across the divide and ran right smack-dab into her. Truck driver's dead and she ain't far behind. Head went through the windshield. They're takin her to University Hospital."

I was stunned, numb. I slowly inspected the CR-V, trying to imagine how the accident happened and the instant terror she must have felt. I saw her blood! The vehicle's front end—the dashboard and windshield—where smashed in past the driver's seat. Even if she lived, it would be a long road to recovery. My Sally would never be the same.

I rushed to the hospital, hoping to embrace and comfort her in her final moments, but she was in the Intensive Care Unit.

"Are you family? Are you her husband?" a stern nurse inquired.

"No," I admitted.

"Then I'm sorry. I can't let you in. She's in such bad shape. She wouldn't even know you were here. Sadly, there's not much we can do for her."

"Is her father here?" I asked. "Maybe I can talk to him. Any friends, relatives?"

"No one's come—no relatives, no friends. I think the police called you and another number in her phone. No one else has come yet."

"Please, Ma'am. You don't understand! Sally's my only hope—I need to see her! You don't understand what she means to me! I can't lose her..."

"I'm sorry, sir. You probably need to go home and get some rest. There's nothing you can do for Sally here. Leave your number at the nurses' desk and go home. Someone'll contact you—I promise."

October 12 – Morning

By the time I got home, I was going on thirty-six straight hours without sleep. My body was fatigued, and my mind was muddled. I'm certain I was in physical shock. I felt nauseous and dizzy, my heart was racing and the skin all over my body was covered with a cold, clammy sweat. I was shivering, but I did not feel cold. I was exhausted, but I could not sleep.

Just like that? How could I have lost her... just like that? When she left my apartment at noon, I was certain I would see her again, though I took seeing her for granted. When she said we needed "take some time away from each other," I knew she didn't mean it. We had plans to go to a movie later.

Of all the doomed relationships I'd ever had in my life, there was a sense of destiny between Sally and me. There were things we were supposed to do together, conversations we were supposed to have, adventures... *and we were supposed to make love.*

Mel knew, so she kept her distance. I could not close my eyes, because every time I did, Sally was there, smiling, and yet I could not keep my eyes open any longer. Struggling against the frailty of my flesh, I succumbed. I collapsed onto the bed, sitting, a half-full snifter of brandy at my fingertips.

I wanted to die to reunite with her. I wanted to follow her, wherever she would go—whatever the cost. Snifter empty, I fell back onto the mattress.

When I awoke, I glanced over to observe the massive fireplace, an enormous log consumed by flames, radiating a sense of serenity and warmth that pervaded the room. The moment was detached from my mortal reality, as there was no point of context. Time and location were irrelevant, though I imagined I was in a cottage on a farm in the remote Norway wilderness during the early 1700s.

As I sat up, I got a better sense of the room and the cottage. A young female lived there, her mother was disabled, missing a foot, and her father, a mercenary soldier and ship builder, was on another conquest on some other continent.

Her uncle did his best to support the family for seven years, but he left for a job in the herring fishery after he had a second child by his Swedish wife. The girl who lived in the cottage and her aging mother, impoverished, struggled to survive, and they would have perished if her father hadn't returned.

I sipped from the chalice of Akvavit left for me on a stand next to the bed, and only then I noticed that I was naked under the warm fur blankets. I closed my eyes and waited. When I opened them, the female from the earlier dream was standing there, smiling. She removed her cloak and unfastened her garments, letting them fall to the floor before getting into the bed with me.

Two bodies morphing into one, we kissed, our mouths an interface, our tingling tongues and lips the bold explorers, eager for adventure. We took our time at introduction, more in preparation, and then finally I breached her secret keep, profound and warm and welcoming, at once conveying near-delirium, a pleasing exercise without restraint.

We knew the movements of the dance, though not by memory or practice, and then finally, release. We lay there, out of breath, both ready to begin again.

I awoke in my own bed at four a.m., disoriented, with a horrible, sick feeling emanating from the pit of my stomach, and then I remembered about the accident. Closing my eyes, I recalled the condition of Sally's silver CR-V, so ravaged in the collision, finally accepting that no one could have survived that crash. If she lived until she got to the hospital, then she died alone and never knew.

Why wasn't her father at the hospital? And where were her family or friends? Despite the time Sally and I spent together, I knew relatively little about her—her personal life, her childhood, family history or life experiences. I didn't even know what kind of work she did. Why hadn't I asked? Now I would never know those things. How had I been so clueless? I wanted to know.

Sitting up, I gradually began remembering the dream—the cottage in the wilderness, the fireplace, the bed... and the female. It was Sally—not by look, but by feel. While making love to her, I was feeling Sally's heartbeat next to mine until both beat as one, until they beat in flawless synchrony. Our inexplicable connection was intense and undeniable.

When the object came into focus on the nightstand, I froze. I could hardly believe my eyes. The female in the dream was wearing a runic ring, and there it was. It was the same ring. The ring that Sally always wore was on the nightstand by the bed. I took it in my hand, squeezing it firmly. What did it mean?

I spent the rest of the day in mourning, mostly drinking brandywine. I wanted to leave the apartment, but where would I go? The world outside would be ever dark with Sally gone. There was a gloom in the sky that threatened to cover even the sun. Mel was hovering, but I didn't feel like writing.

When I called the hospital to see if Sally had survived, a registration clerk told me that she *was* a patient in the Intensive

Care Unit during the previous night, but she was no longer at the hospital. She suggested I check the morgue.

Erick—I remembered that was her father's name. I needed to find him to help locate her body. I needed to hold Sally one last time, weep my tears onto her face, utter unspoken words into un-listening ears. Our story was not over. It was not my ending! She couldn't be alive in one scene and suddenly be gone in the next, leaving us no opportunity for closure! It was my story, not Mel's.

After two dozen calls, I came to the realization that her father had purposely made himself impossible to find, so I went to her condo to see if neighbors had any information about her—yet another dead end. With great trepidation I drove to the morgue, and while I didn't want to know, it would be impossible for me to go forward without knowing.

I cringed after giving the clerk her name, and I was gobsmacked when the medical examiner told me Sally was not at the morgue and her name was not on any recent county death certificate.

I was stunned, though hopeful. I didn't want to go home, because it was a depressing place, and I was not feeling Mel that day. I wanted Sally all to myself in my thoughts. I had my laptop, so I found an all-night café with wi-fi and an available electrical outlet. I was determined to do more research. I had to know.

October 13 – Awakening

The will appears to be strong, strong enough to draw the hugr [animate will] back to one's body. These reanimated individuals were known as draugar. While some versions of the myth say there is no way to kill this vampire, others claim that fire will do the trick. One must lure the draugr back to its tomb and set it ablaze.

I avoided the coffee shop that overcast Saturday morning because the memories were too haunting. Maybe I'd find a new regular spot. I settled for a McCafe Premium Medium Roast from McDonalds and went back to my downtown office to work, but my thoughts kept returning to Sally. Where was she? If not at the hospital or the morgue, then where?

Maybe her father picked her up from the hospital and flew her back to Norway. Was she even an American? Maybe Immigration and Custom Enforcement took her from the hospital.

As a writer, research has always been my forte, along with well-honed powers of observation. An Internet search for "Sally Shippman" turned up a movie actress from the 1940s, with 150 Facebook Sally Shippman profiles, over eighty on LinkedIn and many hundreds more on Google. It was a common name, but "Shippman" wasn't the actual spelling of name from Norway. If I could find that name, perhaps I could find some history on her family to trace it back to her father.

She called her cat "Mama," but she never made any other reference to her mother, whether dead or alive. She never mentioned siblings, relatives or friends. She never told me what kind of work she did.

Ordinarily, I would have asked, but my approach to Sally was different because we communicated in a way I never had with anyone else before. Our relationship was based on a more existential, authentic personal connection where the standard questions mattered less... until she was gone.

I typically avoided Deep Web and Dark Web searches, which contained 500 times more information than standard Internet searches. The Dark Web was a scary place, purposely rigged with dangerous pitfalls and rabbit-holes to prey on the amoral, desperate and naïve. I reluctantly waded in for a few hours—first seeking her family in Norway, and then I focused my attention on draugar.

*****

I took my lunch at 12:30, thinking at first to go to my favorite sushi place five blocks away, but as I passed the coffee shop, something compelled me to stop and go in. My regular lunch there was the turkey and avocado panini sandwich, and as a creature of habit, I ordered and took the table by the window.

Taking Sally's ring from my pocket, I squeezed it in my left hand while I ate.

I usually catch up on the day's news during lunch, so I was steeped in a detailed political analysis about globalism when a chill, beginning at the middle of my back, suddenly crawled out over my skin. What was the expression—*it was as if someone had just walked over my grave.* I could feel a powerful presence, and when I looked up, there she was, smiling, even flirting.

"You haven't called me, and you weren't here yesterday. We have one little fight, and now you're kicking me to the curb?"

I could hardly believe my eyes. It was Sally, standing there without an injury, with not so much as a scratch. I stood so quickly that I knocked over my plate while rushing to embrace her.

"My God, Sally! I'm so glad to see you!" I sighed. "Are you okay?"

"Now *that's* more like it," she joked as she sat and placed her purse on the empty chair. "I'm fine. How are you?"

"Happy to see you! The police called me after the accident. I saw your car. I went to the hospital. You were in Intensive Care! How is this possible?"

"I think you already know the answer to that question," she said, smiling, extending her fingers. "I take it you found my ring?"

I grasped her hand, my fingers shaking as I returned it to its proper place. I studied her carefully... not even a bruise!

"Someone else was driving your car?"

"No, I was driving," she answered, sipping her coffee. "It's a good thing I have full collision with no deductible. I'll get a new car... or maybe a truck this time."

"The ambulance took you to the hospital?" I asked.

"Against my will," she answered. "I wasn't injured... well, maybe a little shaken at first, but I was fine by the time I got to the hospital. No big deal. Basically, a fender-bender."

"And the doctors just let you walk out?"

"Well, once they started looking past the blood, pics and accident reports and actually examined me, they realized I was fine and let me go home."

"Sally," I said, "I saw your car. There is no way you could have been in that crash and walked away. Your car versus a big rig? Officer said fatality rate was 100%. You should be dead now."

"But I'm not," she smiled. "And I thought you'd be *happy* to see me!"

"I am," I insisted. "I just need to understand this. I need you to tell me how it works."

"What works?"

"You're a draugr. Does that mean you're not human?"

"A human relative," she explained. "We are to *homo sapiens* what *homo sapiens* are to *homo erectus*. It's complicated, and there's a lot of misinformation out there. 'Draugr' is just the name and myth that humans came up with for us to breed fear and destroy us."

"So, you're indestructible, immortal?"

"No and yes. Anything can be destroyed if you know how. We're biologically immortal."

"What does that mean?" I asked.

"It means I can die, but I won't die of old age or disease."

"How old *are* you?"

"I was born in Kvikne parish, Hedmark, in Norway on a small farm in the early 1700s, so I guess I'm finishing up my third century."

"So you're three hundred years old?"

"Give or take a few years," she laughed. "Fortunately, I don't look my age, and human time—in hours, days and years—is irrelevant to me. A minute is profound as far as I'm concerned."

"The cottage!" I exclaimed. "The cottage with the big fireplace, the cottage near the forest and stream... and mountains?"

"That's where I was born and grew up."

"How did you make me dream about that?"

"This is starting to sound like an interview," she chided. "We'll have plenty of time to talk about those things later. For now, I've really *missed* you. Come home with me. We'll have dinner and then we'll just cuddle."

October 14 – Yoga and Bath

As I slowly became more convinced of Sally's story, I began to feel inadequate at everything. I had dated women a couple years older than I was, but almost three-centuries-old! I was out of my depth. I'd never be able to say anything she hadn't already heard or share anything she hadn't already experienced.

I was sure she would find everything about me unsophisticated, and whatever education, life experience or wisdom I possessed would be *jejune* in her perspective—like a human adult dating a three-year-old. She had warned me. *Why didn't I run?*

That morning, she suggested yoga and found a peaceful retreat where we could stretch, meditate, have a massage and take a relaxing bath together. I had studied yoga off and on over the last five years, so I was probably at an intermediate level, having mastered a dozen or so poses.

During that time, I had been on retreats, where I practiced *dhyana* (meditation) with a famous yogi from New Zealand. In passing, Sally mentioned she had been practicing *moksha* for one hundred eighty-five years.

To my surprise, our afternoon session was inspiring. Instead of being condescending about my lack of experience, she went out of her way to share techniques, ideas and philosophy. She was reluctant to tell me, but she was actually a *yogini* (divine goddess) who could read and write Classical Sanskrit. After our meditation and massage, we went to the bathhouse for a soak, relaxation and casual conversation.

"The draugar myths I've read about—you said they were misinformation," I began, water swirling before my fingers as I placed a hand on her shoulder. "How much of that, if any of it, is true?"

"Okay," she answered, sitting back, resting her chin on the water's rippling surface. "Are we the re-animated zombies of disgraced warriors? No. Do we live in tombs? No. Do we have weight problems à la Wikipedia? We're simply denser than humans, so we're 15% heavier, weight-to-mass. Denser muscles and denser brains make us stronger and smarter. Human brains have 100 billion neurons—draugar are closer to 120 billion, with 15% more glial cells. Are we greedy, vicious or jealous of humans? Hell-to-the-*No*! Do we smell like death worn over? You tell me."

"Those are all the 'noes,'" I nodded. "Did humans get anything right?"

"Well, we're virtually indestructible, as you now know, but that's due our unique mass and our regenerative science. We can age like humans, but we don't *die* of old age. We get our third set of teeth at about 150 years old, with new sets roughly every hundred years after that. We can enter dreams. We have developed ways to morph into other living forms, though that's irreversible. We travel in unconventional ways, and all of us— we eat humans, but only one per year."

"You *eat* humans?" I repeated, splashing, backing to create distance between us in the three-foot-deep tub. "Is that what happened to you ex? Is that what happened to Rai?"

"Relationship experts say it is never a good policy to discuss an ex while you're on a date."

"Unless he was on the menu," I countered. "Tell me the truth. Did you eat Rai-Rai?"

"Well," she said, closing her eyes in contemplation. "Yes, Rai was consumed," she smiled, seeming to savor the memory, "but it was what he wanted."

"*Right...* Why would he want that?" I asked.

"He couldn't help himself. I tried to push him away, but he just kept on coming, like you... he was relentless, like the moth."

"But if you're not the undead, then why do you eat humans? What would be the purpose of that? Besides, I thought you were vegan."

"I am," she laughed. "You have to know that we're not literally eating humans, not like humans eat a steak or a piece of chicken. There's just something unique about human blood that we need. It used to be worse, when the ancient draugar viciously killed humans, many at a time, and regularly drank their blood.

"Using modern medicine, draugar doctors have over time created a synthetic product that reduces the human blood requirement with modest success, but it wasn't quite enough. For now, each of us needs to consume one human per year. Today is the first day of Gormánuður, our Slaughter Month, and sixteen days before the Seiðr ritual, when we comingle blood."

"Why is consuming blood necessary?" I asked. "What does the blood do to you, or for you?"

"There are some things that humankind will never understand—their expeditions searching for the Garden and the Tree, the Tower and the Narrow Gate, the Key to Human Immortality, the Alchemy of Destiny, the Secret Language of Divinity. Ironically, they've had The Answers all along. The Tree of Life is rooted in their Coursing Blood. The Fountain of Eternal Youth flows from the Human Heart."

"But I don't understand," I continued. "What's so special about human blood?"

"There is a rare, elusive and unstable factor in human blood, stemming from the human heart, that is the key to eternity or perpetual life. Ironically, their blood contains the *Elixir of Life*—no other blood on Earth contains it.

"However, millennia ago, your failing human bodies somehow lost the capability to utilize, metabolize that factor, which resulted in your mortal lives, although our draugar bodies can for immortality. We just don't have that special Human Factor in our blood. Our researchers have spent the last three hundred years at isolating it, and now we're getting close."

"So you *are* not human. Instead, you are undead?"

"Undying, not undead."

"What happens if you don't get fresh human blood?" I asked.

"Then we age, or better put, we start *showing* the effects of aging as a human would. The irony is that, while we won't die of human infirmity or disease, we'll just keep on living, looking older and older. Can you imagine that? Eventually, we look like monsters, and thus the scary stories and myths. In addition to conferring biological immortality, the mysterious human blood component reverses the effects of aging for us—it supplies the factor we lack for eternal youth."

"So it's also about draugar vanity? You don't want to look old?"

"No, it's pragmatism. We can't function in the world if we look like monsters. Humans would target us and hunt us down. Our survival depends on fitting in, and we can't do that without the necessary sacrifice of one human per year for each of us. One day, we hope we won't need humans at all."

"But you're killing humans now!"

"From the perspective of our perpetual lives, they're all going to die anyway. *Homo sapiens* devastated and ravished the *neanderthal*, either forcing them into extinction or absorbing them. It's simply natural selection, but at only one per year, humans have nothing to fear from us."

"How many draugar exist?"

"Maybe 143,000 in a global human population of almost eight billion, or 1/1,000 of one percent, an insignificant number for the benefit humans receive.

"We draugar, because we don't die, are unquestionably the best scientists, doctors and researchers on Earth. The lives we save more than compensate for those that are taken. Our harvesting is more than sustainable."

"Who are the victims?" I asked. "Do you seek out homeless people? Drug addicts? Orphans? Humans who won't be missed?"

She playfully splashed my face with water and wiped her own with a hand towel.

"What?" I complained, laughing.

"Oh, come on! Put yourself in our place. If you had to *eat* someone, would you eat a random, sickly, pissy miscreant, or someone whose blood and liver were contaminated by toxic substances? A frightened child? No, you'd want to eat a vigorous person you know and trust. Mature, healthy, well-adjusted humans provide the greatest benefit."

"Then how do you choose?"

"We don't," she answered then. "Consider nature, where the female spider traps all other prey. She eats the male, but he's the only creature that she doesn't trap, and that's because she doesn't have to trap that compulsive male. He chooses her."

She placed her palms together, bowing slightly, her thumbs indicating the heart chakra. "*Namaste.*"

I repeated the the sober gesture. "*Namaste.*"

By the time we finished the soak, her candid revelations had become almost too much for me to fathom, let alone to believe. I was still perplexed about how she had survived the accident.

"I will never understand, but I don't care. I just want you."

Glancing into her beautiful eyes, I became unconvinced. Simply put, she was the most incredible person I had ever met, but I could not help wondering if I would be her next victim. After all, I did have a choice... at least I thought I did.

*****

We enjoyed dinner at a restaurant near her house, both so relaxed from our intense day that we could barely stay awake.

"In my generation, most draugar who I know and who I kick it with are vegans. We take nutritional supplements, but still, we get the greatest benefit from annual communion." She rolled her eyes. "There are a few exceptions to the rule."

"And the older generations?"

"They have a hard time coping with the pace of change. It's maddening. Many take other forms and live long lives, but those ones eventually die, because that's what they want. Mama loved cats, so she became one. Many of the ancients would rather give up than keep up."

"So are you ready to give up?" I asked.

"Sometimes I want to," she answered. "Eternal life just becomes so predictable and monotonous over time, but you've given me new hope."

I took her left hand in mind, kissing, rubbing it against my face.

"When I thought I lost you, I didn't know what I'd do. I wanted to die. That's when I swore that if I ever had the chance to be with you again, I'd tell you."

"Tell me what?"

I looked into her soft eyes, trying to work up the courage to say what I wanted to say to her from that first day.

"I love you, Sally," I confessed, a tear trailing down my cheek as I fondled the ring on her finger. "For better or for worse, to death—I love you."

Clasping my hands and pulling them close, she wept, kissing them.

"You make me feel so special, baby. I love you, too—more than you will ever understand."

October 15 – They're Everywhere

I awoke that Monday morning feeling re-energized. It was the first full night's sleep I'd gotten in four days. I fell asleep, hoping that she wouldn't visit me in my dreams—but not because I did not want to see her. I just wanted to sleep, to feel alone.

I was still struggling with her explanation of draugar and the idea that she had eaten her last boyfriend. She told me she loved me hours earlier, but was that because she wanted to eat me too? Was that standard practice for draugar?

I put those questions out of my mind because I wanted to invite Sally to the Harvest Festival in the wine country, which was about an hour's drive up into the foothills. I figured we could pack a picnic and visit the popular event, check out vendors, explore the corn maze and try the high-speed sixty-foot-long Zip Line Adventure. It was fun.

Yet something bothered me about her on that day, something different about the way she looked. At first, I thought I was imagining, but there was no mistaking that her skin was darker, and I noted subtle changes in the outline of her eyes. I recognized her face, although her skin and facial aspects seemed "Korean" on that day.

"Another technological advance?" I asked. "Can draugar change ethnicity at will?"

"I wouldn't say entirely at will," she answered me. "It's complicated, meaning much depends on the human DNA that we've acquired through comingling. We've also borrowed from the mimic octopus, the clever little spider of the ocean depths.

"Our early engineers developed genes for sparsely-spaced chromatophores within the dermal layer of our skin, so most of us can change from dark to light complexion using autonomic reflexes, based on various sub-conscious visual cues. Our hair and facial features are the function of an app developed to manipulate genetic phenotyping to a general effect. The long and short of it: we're excellent at camouflage, or blending in."

We were getting a little hungry by one-thirty, so we decided to visit a couple winery tasting rooms before having our picnic on a volcano summit with a descending vineyard vista that stretched on for miles to the horizon. The warm sun was inviting, so we spread out a blanket on the grass, filled our glasses with Semillon and began eating.

Then came the winery cat... directly to Sally, and the picnic was over for me. I sensed a connection between them, which she immediately confirmed.

"She's draugar—one of the ancients."

"So why would she be at an ordinary winery?"

"Why not? It's the perfect life for a cat. Mama just sits around all day. But look at this one—she gets to hunt birds and eat mice all day and let the wine-sippers dote on her. She's well-fed, and damn, the view from here is so spectacular, *n'est-ce pas?*"

"*Incroyable!* How long will she live?"

"One hundred years more or longer perhaps," she said while scratching its belly. "Depends on how long she's been a cat and her physical age before she changed. The human female at the counter said she's been here for nineteen years. She still looks pretty healthy to me."

Next to the semillion bottle was a tin of dirt with the color and consistency of powdered milk chocolate, along with two tiny spoons. I was surprised at how well it accompanied the wine. *Earthy.*

"I've got a question for you," I proposed as I refilled our glasses. "If draugar need blood to stay young, why don't they just feed from a blood-bank, so humans wouldn't have to die?"

"We've tried a number of alternatives to spare human life, but none have worked. To have the necessary benefit, the transfusion of blood must be less than twelve hours old, and it must come from a single living human—at least three and a half liters of whole blood with healthy DNA. No human can lose that much all at once and live. Until researchers find a viable substitute, the sacrifice of one human per year is a necessary evil."

"So draugar are vampires?"

"Vampires don't exist," she answered, "not anymore. It's funny. Humans are entertained watching movies about dinosaurs that no longer exist... and about vampires, or the *nosferatu*, as we called them. They were disgusting, ignorant creatures of the Dark Ages.

"Many of the ancients remember a time when the skies were much darker after a comet exploded within Earth's atmosphere 1,500 years ago. The sun was dimmed for centuries. The *nosferatu* flourished in the twilight that endured for over seven hundred years, but the return of the sun spelled their doom, and they slowly died out. They had their shot, and Nature chose them for extinction. Now, along with dinosaurs, they're the stuff of movies.

"Okay, so draugar *aren't* vampires?"

"They, like *nosferatu*, share some human DNA, but draugar are much more advanced. It's like comparing a moth to an eagle because both can fly."

"And they come from Norway?"

"No, they come from every continent. 'Draugar' is just the name humans in Scandinavia used describe us. It's become generic, like 'vampire' and 'goddess' and 'Coke,' but when you combine human descriptions with local religion and folklore—mythologies are born.

"The Ewe people of west Africa called us the *adze,* but we were the *jiangshi* in Asia. Croatian men feared the *morana,* and the gypsies named us *mullo.* Humans have assumed we're vampires, but then again, humans once assumed that spiders were insects and whales were fish. Draugar is also the name of the research and medical facility we use today."

"How does it work?" I asked. "Do draugar actually eat the blood?"

"They did long ago, but that practice was messy, cruel and inefficient. In the early twentieth century, draugar researchers discovered that a fresh four-liter transfusion three times a year would do the trick. Then they began experimenting with increasing the lifespan of the red blood cells we consume, which they were able to extend from 120 days to 360 days, which got the process down to one three-and-a-half-liter blood exchange per year."

"How old is the oldest draugr?"

"The oldest I know?" she said, "I'd say just over sixteen hundred years, but some will tell you there's an actual three-thousand-year-old draugr who's on the verge of transcending tangibility. Because they can't adapt, most of the ancients decide to end life at about seven hundred years, which coincides with the onset of natural telepathy. That's telling. Some give up while comingling and never wake. It gets to be too much. Others just morph to become long-lived animals, like this cat, living out their last days at peace with nature. Me, I've always thought I'd like to be an eagle. It's a popular choice."

"Does the blood have to be compatible?"

"The DNA—that's the most important thing. The blood-type has to match, but the DNA-type has to be complementary—at least 90% complementary. And just so you know—you and I are a great match. We're possibly closer than anyone I have ever met. I could smell your DNA-type and sense your distinctiveness the moment we touched. It's uncanny, really."

"So you want to eat me?"

"Your choice. I'll feed, or comingle, because I must, but it doesn't have to be you. Unless you're different than the others, you will beg me to eat you, to absorb you. Unless you're different, I'll comply."

"Rai begged you?"

"More than all the rest. It didn't work out, but I had absorbed components of his DNA over the year before he died, which means he will always be a part of me—even when you and I are together."

"Do you only eat men?"

"It's easier for me that way, though others choose according their preferences related to self-identity. I've been comingling for better than 250 years, and so for me there must be some meaning, usually involving some religious or a ritual significance—since otherwise, there is no growth. It is essential that I know who I'm consuming, though beyond that end, it is important I *love*, or tolerate that person, since he will become a part of me—his health, his thoughts, his will.

"Most of the younger draugar feel that way—they want to leave a spotless bio-footprint—harvesting the non-essentials in ways that prove sustainable. We don't eat kids or parents or custodial providers and restrict ourselves to healthy adult non-essentials—mostly self-indulgent males. Thus, we take no one who really matters in the greater scheme of things"

"Thank you. It's good to know I don't matter."

"Let's be fair now. You've fashioned yourself as a private person, accountable to no one," she countered. "You have no attachments. If you were gone tomorrow, who would miss you?"

"Mel would miss me," I answered without thinking, considering her in the equation for the first time.

"Mel? The female you were seeing? You never told me about Mel."

"She's female, but she's not a human female. Mel's my Muse."

"Your Muse?" Sally laughed. "Ah, Melpomene—the tragic Muse. She isn't real. Your imagination makes her real to you. She's just a part of your creative process. You conjured her."

"No, she chose me, and she lives within my writing space. She won't let me die."

"Really?" she asked, her face concerned. "Then I'd love to meet her."

"You already have—at my apartment, and you were in fatal car accident three hours later."

*****

It was a long afternoon of flirtation, ruse and discovery. By the end of the day, I was a believer, but I was certain Sally wasn't telling me everything. I was intellectually outmatched, though I believed we were ideally suited—two parts of a single being.

At her condo, we sat to finish another bottle of wine, Mama on my lap.

"Do you recognize them when you see them... even as animals?"

"They're everywhere. Before it's over, you'll learn to recognize them too."

"How do you reproduce? Can you have children?"

"If circumstances are just right I could, though I'm not counting on it. What you really want to ask is *by being intimate with me, could you become draugar?*"

"No," I answered, "although yes, I do."

"Of course you'd answer *yes*. The question was inevitable," she said while moving Mama to her side and pressing her firm body close to mine. "You're drawn inescapably to me, as moth to flame. The compulsion to connect with me consumes you every minute of your day."

"Yes..."

"If we comingle our bodies and our blood, I'll absorb your DNA, but then you'll be infected with our draugar DNA, a viral vector with potential for our biological immortality. Unfortunately, the blood exchange kills 98% of the humans who are intimately exposed.

"After I consume you, you'll have only a 2% chance of becoming draugar. *Strait is the gate, and narrow is the way, which leadeth unto life, and few there be that find it.*" She gently kissed my lips, her hand trailing down my chest. "I know you want to comingle."

"But we've already comingled... in my dreams. You were there. We felt it."

"We've felt the lure of what compatible comingling could be," she teased, "but such a union is more tantalizing in the flesh, and very soon, you'll have to choose."

October 16 – Immortality

Eventually, it made sense why Sally was good at every facet of life we explored together. As far as I could determine, she was a yogini, a surgeon, an oil painting master, a judo black belt, a computer hacker, an opera soprano (who had a brief and meaningless affair with Wolfgang Amadeus Mozart), a marine biologist, an Olympic-level competitor at dressage and stadium jumping, an executive chef ranging over the world's cuisines, a chiropractor, a sexual therapist, a master sommelier, a ballerina, a hematologist, a concert cellist, a quantum physicist, a jazz composer, a virtuosic violinist, a psychologist, and she admitted to twenty-five PhDs and other advanced university degrees. She really was a force of nature.

She pushed on her right outside edge, made a right forward outside three-turn, Choctaw step, forward outside edge, three-turn, Choctaw, forward outside edge, outside three-turn. Perfect form, perfect pattern, perfect outside figure eight. We were ice skating at the mall right after the Zamboni finished resurfacing the rink, and Sally, as usual, outperformed the best of humans. We went to dinner at a vegan sushi house.

"The day after your accident," I began, "I looked for you. I know you work, but you never told me what you do."

"Work?" she laughed. "I volunteer at a no-kill, cage-free pet sanctuary that I own. I'd hardly call it work. I get to visit with my kitties all day, along with a few old friends."

"So how do you get by, moneywise?"

"Money is irrelevant when you have wealth," she answered. "Are you forgetting I'm almost three centuries old? I married well—four times, a long, long time ago. It helps when you can outlive entire families. Think about the interest alone. My wealth is spread out over vast territories and time. I imagine I'm among the upper one-percent of one-percenters, but money's immaterial when time is irrelevant, and thus the curse of immortaltiy. My cats mean more to me."

"It isn't fair," I argued, "the advantages draugar have over humans. They're not innately smarter or better—they just live longer."

"A distinct benefit in an ephemeral world," she smiled. "It took me five years to become fluent in Mandarin and Cantonese, three years for Russian and Shoshoni. I'm fluent at over forty-five languages, and I've experienced hundreds of cultures, including Native American life before Europeans arrived. I've attended college for over ninety-five years, but who's counting. It helps when you have all the time in the world. Incidentally, our brains are denser, so we actually *are* smarter than humans."

"But draugar are dependent on human society," I argued then, "with its schools, technology and wealth. You need humans. Without them, draugar would be no different than other long-lived organisms on the planet, like turtles. Some bristlecone pines are five thousand years old—three times the age of the oldest draugar. Without human society, their blood and DNA, draugar would age past recognition and relevance. They'd go the way of the vampires."

"We won't always be dependent on humans," she countered. "One day very soon, our researchers will find a way to isolate, analyze and replicate that unique factor in human blood, and on that day, humans will no longer be necessary."

"What happens then?"

"When we attain inherent immortality? When we no longer are dependent on inferior humankind?" she asked while sipping from the cloudy sake in her glass. "Who knows? Some draugar are determined to subdue the Earth as queens and princesses. They want to force the human females to submit and execute the males."

"Inherent immortality? Wouldn't that be more like artificial life? Maybe nature selected the draugar for extinction as well, but you're using science to change fate and cheat destiny. What are the words? *Hugr* and *munr*? Spirit and mind—a strong will to live that overcomes the frailty of the *líkami*—the body?"

"I can see you've been doing your homework," she smiled. "Wikipedia this time? The reality is that biological immortality on a corporal earth sometimes feels doomed. Draugar have the potential of everlasting existence, but in the end, many realize that physical life must end for the purpose of context and meaning."

"You mean life gets boring after hundreds of years?" I asked. "So much for immortality!"

"It's not that," she answered. "You just get tired sometimes, tired of the temporary nature of every other living thing on the planet. Do you know how hard it is for any of us to have a long-term relationship?"

"Well, your relationships would last longer if you weren't eating your partners."

"I've tried it the more traditional way," she said, "where I didn't tell my mates what I was... *and* I didn't eat them. I even let myself age so that the experience would seem real to them, but that way was never real to me. It was either 'live a lie' or tell them what I was. It's never worked out well."

"And when you told your mates what you were?" I asked. "When you were completely honest with them?"

"Then they *wanted* me to eat them. They chose to risk exchanging blood and DNA, so they could live perpetual life with me. They all died... too many to count. But what's a girl to do?" she said, taking up a brandy snifter half-full of cognac. Her painful tears of sorrow melted my heart.

"Maybe you just haven't met the right guy?"

"Do you know how many times I've heard that cheesy line?" she sighed, disgusted. "And in how many languages? Live a few hundred years, and you'll realize how utterly clueless most human males are. Female humans should be classified as a separate, more-evolved species."

"I can see biological immortality has made you cynical."

"No, but I'm tired of pretending—pretending to be naïve, helpless and submissive. I'm tired of hiding the fact that I know more than the all the arrogant human males I've ever dated... about everything!

"I'm tired of losing competitions and debates to them on purpose, pretending to be surprised by their sophomoric insights and antics, and listening to them drone on and on about subjects they don't understand, *and* not kicking their sorry asses when they try to pull that silly macho act on me.

"I'm tired of their inattention to detail, their *dick-brains* and their stupidity... and not being on top. Male-missionary— it's the only way! Take it from a female who's *really* been around. One hundred percent of human males *suck* in bed. Females deserve to be on top!"

"Feel better now?" I asked.

"That's why when you asked me to name my greatest regret, I said 'immortality.' Perpetual existence in a corporal, mortal world means you do the same things over and over— damned to have the same conversations, the same arguments, the same pain—only the resentment grows, unless you have an echo."

Tears overwhelmed her eyes. Blinking them back, she swigged another warm mouthful of cognac and continued.

"Eternity alone is virtual Hell. I'm so jealous of humans, who live short, relatively meaningful lives, and then they get to die. Only when looking back from death does life take on meaning. There must be a conclusion, a period at the end of the sentence, the last page of the book. Otherwise, you are nothing *more* than a force of nature."

Within her eyes I sensed such solitude, the loneliness and the blur of centuries passed.

"You're right. Artificial life belongs in an artificial environment," she sobbed. "Maybe instead of eating you, I'll just become a cat and live with you."

"But I'm mortal. I'll die someday..."

"Before you do, you'll take me to my no-kill, cage-free pet sanctuary, where I have friends and can live out the last pages of my book."

Clearly, the alcohol had taken its toll. Sally was drunk, so I paid the bill and drove her home, where we made-out on the couch for two hours before I returned to my senses and went home.

October 17 – Interracial Relationship

I spent the morning researching immortality, which led to a re-examination of Christianity and its promise of perfect health, everlasting life, eternal peace and happiness. Sally had perfect health and biological immortality, but she seemed deeply discontent.

She said most draugar choose to take mortal forms after seven hundred years. They ultimately choose death over biological immortality. Why could they not find happiness? Obviously, Sally wasn't accurately sharing draugar vulnerabilities with me.

Compared to me, she was omniscient, which had been overwhelming in the beginning. She told me she and her father were travelling in France when the Treaty of Paris was signed, which ended the French and Indian War, and they were in London when British Parliament passed the Stamp Act—the first direct tax on the American colonies.

In 1792, she entered her second marriage to a wealthy businessman in Shanghai, where she was a popular calligraphy artist. While she was initially intimidating—seventeen days into the relationship, I was over it.

*****

The final step in dispatching the draugr was to burn the remains to cold ashes and then bury the ashes in a remote spot or throw them out to sea: only then was the undead truly dead and destined to rise no more (Ellis-Davidson, Road to Hel, pp. 37-38).

I felt guilty as I drove because I spent the last hour researching draugar vulnerabilities. On the Dark Web, I found pages from an ancient tome that said the surest way to kill a draugr was decapitation or burning. I wouldn't allow myself to even imagine harming Sally, but Mel did.

In the comments section, one person suggested Hollywood actress Jayne Mansfield was a draugr, and additional comments outed other draugar popular figures... like Vladamir Putin.

*****

When I arrived at the reservoir, Sally was standing at the beginning of the fish ladder, waiting for me.

"You were looking up ways to kill me?" she huffed, arms crossed. "Don't lie!"

"I was doing research on draugar like you asked," I answered defensively. "What makes you say that?"

"I can see it on your face. Come on... you imagined doing it to me when our eyes met."

"Stop messin with me. You told me draugar can't read minds—not until they're seven hundred years old, so you're just fishin."

"Would you bet your life on it?"

As we walked up the slope next to the fish ladder, a huge king salmon leapt three feet clear of the water and splashed into the turbulence of the next liquid step. We stopped to watch other fish follow suit.

"The sun's a little intense out, so I think I'll be African American today," she said. The change was instantaneous. She was still Sally definitively, but she was black... and she was beautiful.

"Seriously?" I asked, astonished, hardly believing my eyes.

"How you like me now?" she laughed.

"Uh, this is a hatchery," I said, shaking my head, adjusting to the change in her appearance. "These female fish are being harvested for their eggs and flesh. You're a vegan. Why would you want to come here?"

"I come here every year for the symbolism. *Oncorhynchus tshawytscha*, by human definition. These females are at the end of their life cycle. They're semelparous, meaning they mate once, and then they die. It's one of nature's reoccurring themes, more so for males."

"The impulse in males to mate," I said aloud, lusting her with my eyes, "it's very powerful."

"Impulse?" she laughed. "These fish know nothing about mating. They know nothing about what they're getting into, what they're in for. Do you really think they abuse their bodies, defeat rivers and swim up waterfalls because they're eager to get laid in the cool pool at the top?" she said, laughing louder.

"They have no idea why they're doing what they're doing and no clue that the pool and what awaits them is even *up* there!"

"It's instinct. They're not thinking. They're following their programming."

"So is it truly *free will*?" she asked.

"Will involves thinking, contemplation," I answered. "They don't have to figure out how to leap over waterfalls. They just do it."

"How are humans any different?"

"Humans think," I argued.

"*Humanity* thinks, but humans follow their programming, their impulses, like the salmon," she countered. "It's part of nature's engineering. Consider the ant—does a single ant with a grain of sand in its mandibles ever contemplate the greater reality? Yet ordinary ant cities rival the greatest human cities. Humans, like ants, possess a form of *collective* intelligence, making technology and engineering possible, but individually, humans are not capable of contemplating anything beyond the parameters of their intrinsic programming."

"You mean 'most' humans?" I insisted.

"I mean *all* humans, even their so-called intellectuals, who are fond of thinking they have thoughts. Individual human knowledge is silly, but as a species or race, humans do possess a sort of innate genius, like ants and termites."

"Mate and die?" I wondered distinctly. "Are you saying that if I 'comingle' with you, I'll die?"

"Male spiders and men, male moths and men—male salmon—it's your place in the ecosystem."

"If humans are so unworthy," I asked, "then why do you date them? Why don't you date your own race? Why aren't you dating a draugr?"

"Male humans are intolerable in most cases," she answered, "but just think about a human-like male creature, hundreds of years old—testosterone working in overdrive! It's genetically unfeasible, but show me a draugr male, and I'll show you the earth's worst asshole, my own father notwithstanding—it's why Mama became a cat."

"Oh, so have you ever dated a draugr?"

"Yes, briefly, but he wasn't fully draugr at the time. I'd never date a draugr male, though they're very rare. I've always sought out authenticity, so that would be impossible. But just imagine what a life that you and I could have if *you* became a blood-comingled draugar male! All I've ever wanted is a male that I could mold and train."

"So you think you're training me? Well, maybe I'm training you! What are you training me to do?"

"To survive."

We ascended the fish ladder ramp, stopping at a place where the watery stairs were much more challenging. Many of the fish were defeated on successive attempts and waited to rebuild stamina and resolve.

"What are we?" I asked.

"On an adventure," she answered.

"No, I mean *what is our relationship*? Are we dating? Are we a couple?"

"You disservice the significance of my answer by your silly question," she tisked. "Of *course* we're in a relationship!"

"Are you my girlfriend? Are we lovers?"

"After I come see you tonight, you let me know. I do love you."

"What about Rai? Did you love him the same way you love me? Is our relationship more special?"

"Rai made a choice," she answered, "and he wasn't up to the reality of that choice. He, more than anyone else over all these years, is the cause of my cynicism."

"Why do you date outside your race?" I asked. "Don't you consider humans as inferior?"

"Race is a human term that defies logic. All humans, black, white, brown and in-between are of the same race. The idea of human races is ridiculous and exploitable. Just look at the color of my skin today.

"Think about it. A dog can have puppies in many colors and hues, but they're the same dogs! They aren't different breeds, based on color or hair. A pity the same doesn't happen with humans! Nonetheless, dishonest draugar and humans use that concept, the social construct of race, to keep the masses divided. So long as the carefully-conjured subsets are enemies or adversaries, humans will never turn on us or on their human rulers. 'Draugar' are the only extant separate human-like race."

"I'm human," I asserted. "You know more than I do. You're smarter than I am, and stronger. You are distinctly aware of that, so why would we be lovers?"

"Because I've spent my lifetime trying to find my echo, and every time I've called, there's been no answer—not until I met you. You're different, and I've never said these words to any male before you: *you will be my final male, my last and only chance.*"

At the top of the ladder, hatchery workers netted the fish. Using medical scalpels, some slit open the females' abdomens and ripped out the bright orange eggs while others caught the males by the tails and squeezed the cloudy milt out over the eggs.

"Loki's retribution," she snarked, in a daze. "It's one of the reasons I come up here. Loki tricked the Höðr into killing his brother, Baldr. Then he jumped into a river and transformed himself into a salmon to escape punishment from the other gods. No one could catch him until Thor grabbed him by the tail, which is why the salmon's tail is tapered. It's like watching him die, over and over."

"You really want me to become a draugr?" I asked.

"You are inferior... for now," she answered, "but you will transform over time. If you survive our comingling, then I will finally have my echo, and we'll be able to share perpetual life as lovers. Together, we can have children and we can pursue knowledge of good and bad and the true purpose of life in blood and flesh."

October 18 – Mel

Years ago, Mel shared a story through me about a youth from 14th-century Japan. His clan loved education, while a rival clan loved warfare. In a final clash, the war clan destroys the intellectuals, leaving the youth bitter and eager to abandon weaker spirits over a more violent philosophy.

He is welcomed at the edge of the enemy camp by a powerful *Oni*, or goddess, who takes him into the tent of the shogun lord and directs him toward the master's bloody weapon.

"*Take up his sword,*" she says to him, "*and then your destiny!*"

The young man then takes up the blade and lops off the shogun lord's head and with it follows the *Oni* into the camp where she names him the new warlord king. He becomes powerful and eventually takes a wife, only to find her strangled in the marriage bed on the morning after the wedding night. After a second wife suffers the same misfortune, the *Oni* tells the shogun lord that he can never take a fleshly wife because the *Oni* is his spirit wife until he dies.

Yet over time, the shogun meets a fleshly female who he realizes is the echo in his life, a beautiful female from Portugal, whose Christian faith intimidates his *Oni* spirit wife. Knowing that the *Oni* will seek out and then influence some unwitting wise and foolish slave to kill the fleshly female who he loves, he takes her as a wife, but on the wedding night, he drugs her with a potent potion and he sends her back to Portugal for her protection her enemy.

Angry, the *Oni* abandons the shogun on the battlefield, casting him into the sea of fate. Steeled by experience on the battlefield, he remains in power for many years before the *Oni* brings an ambitious, spirited young and foolish boy into his tent where he sleeps.

"*Take up his sword,*" she says to the boy, "*And then your destiny!*"

*****

It was one of the many stories I wrote while seated next to Mel. I met her when I was an ambitious young and foolish boy, and the "sword" I inherited was Mel herself, though I did not know my unfortunate benefactor. I knew her as "Melpomene, the favored Muse of Solomon." While I could feel her next to me, imagination made her real—real enough to see, real enough to hear, real enough to even touch. The soul-inspiring songs she sang sustained me in my work.

Her skin was the color of aged honey, while her crown of wavy dark black tresses was pulled back and tied in braids. Her eyes were dark, exotic and mischievous and she smelled of vanilla, cinnamon, frankincense and myrrh—there was unmistakable divinity in the design of her face. She was always dressed in colorful, flowing robes. Her voice was deep, alluring.

But Mel was cruelly possessive. She was the reason that I was never successful at relationships with human females and the reason that my only life's endeavor has been writing. She was always at my side when I was in my writing space, always urging me to stay, to spend another hour, to start another story, and often I was helpless to resist.

When I was writing thrillers, sometimes I would work for seven days or longer without sleep. And after finally asleep, I would awaken to read pages I distinctly did not remember writing.

"I do not like this foolish girl who is distracting you. She represents a threat to all that we have planned. Be warned—she's dangerous, a threat to all we've worked to publish to the world. She lies and schemes to trap you in a web, where you will not escape. Be wise and stay away from her."

"She's different, intriguing, but she's hardly dangerous," I said. "She knows about you, Mel, and she does not believe that you are real. She thinks I conjured you."

"She's lying, since she understands an ordinary human cannot choose in matters of divinity. She knows why I have chosen you."

"She isn't human. I'm convinced of that. She's of a separate draugar race that feeds on humankind while hiding in plain sight."

"You can't have both of us. Reject her while you can, or it will be too late."

*****

My writing space was important to me, so it was a set-aside, a particular room that could never change, where everything had a place—every pen, every sheet of paper, the coffee cup, the brandy decanter, the cigar humidor, the computer, the music player, the fan, the candles—every item in the room was in its proper place—and there could be no dust.

I've never tolerated humans in my writing space because they're curious, creating dust and moving things. So as I sit to write, no thing was out of place, so as I sat, there was no time, and then I'd see the gate, the entrance to "the writing zone."

Mel was always in her proper place beside me as I wrote. While words are composed of letters, letters do not exist in that zone and were given no consideration. Words did not exist, and neither did sentences or paragraphs. Skilled writers were able to capture thoughts, geniuses could write in ideas, but only the truly inspired could write in concepts. There, in that zone, I loved Mel, and she loved me.

I never dated in high school or college because Mel was so overwhelming. At twenty-three and under pressure from friends and relatives, I attempted a relationship with a human woman. It was awkward and ultimately ended because she wanted me to choose: "It's either me or your writing." I didn't date again for six years, but I was constantly writing.

Many human females had been fascinated by my life as a writer, but it has always come down to competition and choice, and Mel hadn't helped. The inescapable choice: writing or women. I had a short-lived marriage to a human female who I loved, but she didn't stand a chance against Mel, who sabotaged the relationship and drove her out of my life.

Sally was different. She was the only fleshly woman I had ever met who could hold her own against Mel. Sally had become my obsession.

"I have a question for you," she said as we had dinner at her condo. "Don't take this the wrong way. I like having you over. You're here almost every night, but is there some reason why you've only invited me to your place one time?"

"No. I'm just not used to entertaining there. I'm sorry."

"Why? And I ask that question to ask, 'what you're hiding there... or *who* are you hiding?' We're a couple, right? We're in a relationship?"

"Yes, but you don't need an invitation to come over... unless there's something to the urban legend about vampires, or maybe draugar 'having to be invited in...'"

"Very funny," she sighed, rolling her eyes. "You do realize I can go there any time—into your space, so if you're hiding something, I'm bound to find out what or who it is. Is it Mel?"

"Mel is Mel. She's part of my writing," I shrugged, a bit distrustful. "Come on! She isn't real—I conjured her! Don't tell me you're jealous?"

"I'm not jealous," she answered, "but when I'm in a relationship, I don't share. One web—one spider. We owe each other complete honesty and loyalty. Do you love me?"

"Yes."

"Then it's me or Mel? It's binary. Since humans aren't capable of choice, I'll just have to decide for you."

October 19 – You Don't Know Me

During the early evening, we were at a karaoke bar at Union Square, near the San Francisco tenderloin. Fortunately, Sally chose a song I knew, but I was uneasy as I waited for my pick-up cue in our duet. I was certain I was outmatched, and yet I sang, living the lyrics, emoting from my heart.

> *You give your hand to me,*
> *And then you say hello,*
> *And I can hardly speak,*
> *My heart is beating so.*
> *And anyone could tell,*
> *You think you know me well,*
> *But you don't know me.*

She smiled and winked, pretending to be impressed, and responded in perfect pitch, with a distinctive R&B flair.

No, you don't know the one,
Who dreams of you at night,
And longs to kiss your lips,
And longs to hold you tight,
To you I'm just a friend,
That's all I've ever been,
But you don't know me.

When I began again, the once-loud, bustling bar was quiet, still, with everyone's attention focused on the stage, but more specifically on Sally. Staring lovingly into her eyes, I never sang a better verse, while finishing to raucous applause.

An eager, awe-inspired line formed at our table, not allowing us to sit. Most complimented our ability, while some were certain that we were celebrities One female lingered in the background, brazenly approaching when we were alone.

"From blocks away, I heard a whigger-white-chick's pitchy over-singing, Sally, or whatever name you're using now, but I knew instantly that it was you."

My date's revulsion to the shapely woman standing there in tight black jeans and a revealing haltertop was obvious. And looking from the *femme fatale* with blue-black hair, long fingernails and make-up, then to Sally, who was so conservative, I could not help but wonder who she was.

A handsome twenty-something man had followed her, his eyes like glass, and looking back at him, she sighed, disgusted. Turning angrily, she dragged a sharpened nail across his forehead until it bled bright red, and after tasting of the blood on her finger, she grabbed a handful of his hair and sneered.

"Unworthy, but I'll let you grovel at my feet for now. So on your knees! And kiss my toes, unworthy human male!"

Within an instant, he obeyed, forgetting all convention as he crawled on hands and knees. He kissed her ankles, grunting like a carnal creature, smacking as he reached her naked toes. His frantic fingers groped her legs and thighs, and finally her ass. She watched him for a moment in disgust, then leered at me and slammed her sexy shoe and foot into his face to send him flailing, tumbling across the room.

"Now go away or you will *die* tonight!"

"You said you'd be in Kazakhstan," an irritated Sally carped aloud. "If I had known that you'd be anywhere near San Francisco, then I never would have come to California in October for this year."

"You chose California, just like every other year," the scary woman said. "Who's the new meat? Aren't you going to introduce me? Don't be crass."

Sally took a contemplative breath, annoyed, and finally she sighed. "This is my older sister, whom we call Astrid," reluctantly she said to me. "We're leaving now!"

"That was my name in French," Astrid responded, "and it was reserved for only family... and lovers whom I chose. We all have many names," Astrid continued, ogling me, her eyes examining my body, stopping at my groin. "The name I go by now: Rhianna—or Queen Anna, if you will."

She slinked into the chair by me and grabbed my thigh, and then she slid her hand along my body, briefly stopping at my crotch, until she reached my chest. She reveled when I shuddered as she took my hand, examining my palm. She licked from wrist to fingertips. "Love the way you lie, Sis."

"We have to leave now!" Sally warned, nervous, grabbing my hand. "Come on!"

"Oh, I see!" the seeming younger woman said, smacking her lips, her soft, warm palm pressing on my chest, holding me against the seat back. "He's *very* compatible! I'd say he's maybe even 98%. You've done well this year, *putain*. You *do* know how to pick the good ones—*even when you do it on your own*."

Then she turned to me. "Has my sister told you that she plans on *eating* you? Or is she pretending she's the perfect little girlfriend, and what you've got going on with her is real?"

She leaned toward me and licked my face. I tried to pull away, but she was incredibly strong. I couldn't move as she licked the other side and laughed. "Do you know what she is, you idiot?"

"She's a draugr," I strained, uncomfortable with the woman's strength, spicy parfum-like essence, warm saliva and aggression.

"She's a whore, a treacherous conniving whore. Dear little boy, you taste so yummy I could eat you now, right here and now!" she whispered. "She's a draugr? Really? Did my sister truly tell you *that*? So does she play the honest, chaste, and tragic draugr role this time? And did she say you were her last and only chance, her *final male*? You're such an imbecile! It's all an act, since everything she's told you is a lie. My sister doesn't care a thing about you, fool. She only wants to eat you. Then when she's sated, she will find another fool a year from now."

"That's not true," Sally argued before shoving her sister back in the chair. Her face turned dark before she bared her teeth, her face resembling a threatened, predadory feline, hissing loud enough to scare the people in the neighboring vicinity. "Now back off, Báthory! He's mine!"

"You see?" her sister laughed. "See what I told you? You better run away, you petty ant... unless already it's too late. *Mais ooh-la-la*—has she been boinking you while in your dreams, *petit garçon*? Is she preparing you for death in the comingling?"

"I love Sally," I protested, "and she loves me. She's told me everything. I know the risks involved, and I'm still here."

"You are such a jive turkey!" Astrid sighed sarcastically, "and your defending her is foolishness. If you understand everything, then why would you believe an explanation from someone who *tells* you she wants to eat you? Yet you seem slightly intelligent. Why would a spider ever advertise to a foolish ant... that a web *is* a web?"

"I've done my own research."

"Such a smart one this time, my little strumpet sister!" she laughed, winking at Sally before turning back to me. "It seems you know how to use Wikipedia, or maybe you have played a few male-dominated puerile video games? Well, I'm gonna let you in on a little secret: *almost none of the draugar stuff on the Internet and in those games is true!*"

"I went beyond the Internet," I argued then. "I went to the Dark Web."

"Oooh!" she mocked, "the *Dark* Web! And why do you think they call it the Dark Web, little boy? Who do you think *manipulates* the Dark Web? Who created the Dark and the

Deep Web, which is only a miniscule part of the *Real* Web? which you've somehow managed to stumble into. *Un petit garçon si tentant!*[4]"

"I said we're leaving!" Sally growled, standing, snatching my arm. "As you can see, not all draugar make the most of the gift and privilege of perpetual life."

Astrid only laughed while kicking her stiletto-clad, pedicured feet up on the table top.

"My quixotic sister—forever seeking out the *Radical*, which cannot and will never exist. He's cute, Sis, but he's not the one—I tasted him. No human born can change the web of Destiny.

"Listen, you puny little simpleton," she said to me, "she's been my younger sister for two hundred ninety-three odd years—a child, always Miss Perfect, such a dedicated 'Daddy's-Girl'—but that's an act that got old and tired when she betrayed me. She's a phony and conniving backstabber. Don't believe anything she tells you!"

*****

"Her name was Mary Tudor in one life, and Countess Báthory in another life, I swear! She's a cold-blooded killer!"

Sally ranted on about her sister and her "failed and wasted lives" for most of the way home. She compared Astrid to Loki, calling her a bitter, malicious drama queen, addicted to chaos. Kissing my hand, she assured me that our love and everything we experienced were real. When I briefly glanced over at her, I was touched by her genuine tears.

*****

We were seated on her couch when she asked me if I wanted to come up to her bed. I was surprised, because she had never invited me to her bed before. She pulled back the blanket, stripped down to her underwear and encouraged me to do the

---

[4] French – *Such a tempting little boy!*

same. Between the sheets, her naked skin against mine produced immediate arousal, which was obvious.

"We won't be having sex," she announced indifferently, "since now is not the time, though nonetheless, we need to 'talk of sex.'"

"To *talk* of sex?" I asked

"When was the last time you were sexually engaged?"

"Physical sex? I'm embarrassed to admit it, but it's been about three years," I answered, reflecting that I had always found it hard to be intimate with human females. It was awkward and messy, sometimes involving earthy, carnal odors. "Does it matter that it's been so long?"

"I have to warn you then, that carnal sex with me will definitely exceed all pleasures you have ever known, surpassing any sensory enjoyment you have ever felt, and that's an understatement. You won't find out about *that* on the Dark Web or in video games!"

As I reflected on my research into draguary, I realized there was never mention of their sexuality.

"But how will it be different?" I asked, intrigued though nervous right away.

"Just think about it—a twenty-eight-year-old body with over 280 years of sexual experience. I am expertly-practiced in many long-forgotten sensual techniques that are forbidden because the exhilaration has proven too much for humans to endure. Human males have a pain threshold, but they also have a pleasure threshold. *La petite mort*[5] *peut etre une chose dangereux.*[6]"

"You mean sex with you would *kill* me?"

"Well, once the pleasure threshold is exceeded," she presaged, "the risk is higher for acute ventricular tachycardia—for rapid and uneven coronary action, which in many cases, leads to prolonged coma or to death. I'll need to prepare you."

"And what does that involve?" I asked.

"I need for you to go back home and wait for me tonight. I'll come to visit in your dreams, and we'll begin intensive

---

[5] French — *The Little Death*, idiom for "an orgasm"

[6] French – *An orgasm can be a dangerous thing*

training in the sexual arts. I'll teach unique technique that you will need to know if you will live beyond comingling, since lucid dreaming will reduce the risk. Take this," she said, while handing me a bottle of Akvavit from her cellar room. "Its quality is pharmaceutical. You'll want to drink two ample shots before you go to bed, since it will help you to survive."

"Okay," I said, taking the bottle. "Is this the part where I should be scared?"

"You should be looking forward to it. Tonight, we find your pleasure threshold. Welcome to my web!"

October 20 – Assassination

Then I awoke, though groggy and unsettled as I rose. At first, I couldn't tell exactly where I was. Yet wait! Somehow the room had changed. And glancing to the nightstand, there it was: the runic ring. I slowly started to remember what I dreamt... or lived. The bed was different—the walls, and ceiling too.

I found myself within the cottage in the winter scene. A massive, crackling fire warmed the rustic wooden room with carved-out sconces, all along the walls—each with a flickering candle, subtly illuminating shadows in the light, and then the pale and supple flesh, a female body swaying rhythmically while straddling my body on the bed.

My eyes still closed, I took a breath, recalling, savoring the feminine, distictive carnal scent, which emanated and originated from the warm and silky sheen of dampness covering her glistening skin—a sensual and pheromone-inspired mélange of provocative aromas, overpowering and purposed to entice.

So graceful in her rhythmic ritual, it seemed a dance to music so ethereal that I could almost hear the faint percussion in my mind. It began a stirring, tingling sensation deep within my entrails, a trembling impression, causing me to fear that they'd be sucked into a void. My senses overwhelmed, I helplessly relented, losing consciousness.

When next I was awake within the trance or dream, the female was beside me with her arms embracing me. Her legs were

also clamped around me, while her practiced thumbs and
fingers—sliding, rubbing and manipulating, found their frets
along my spine. My body was a sensual violin within the expert
clutches of a luthier, or better yet, a virtuosic soloist. I felt a
gentle pop, and then the came a flood of pleasure, unimaginable,
in waves that built to synchrony, and then I felt "sensation of
freefall," which lingered and endured until the room dissolved to
nothingness.

I took the ring from the nightstand and gripped it in my hand as, closing my eyes, I savored the dream. It was more than a dream. She seemed so tangible. Taking a deep breath, I realized that even the parfum from her body had remained, atomized, suspended in the sticky air. Sally had definitely been in that room with me. *More than a dream!*

I noticed it when I entered the kitchen to make tea. Something felt different. For the first time since I could remember, I couldn't feel her. *Mel?* I went immediately to my office, unlocked it and slammed open the door.

Right away, I saw that my desk and chair were missing. My laptop had been moved to the leather couch. The brandy set was gone, all the music was gone, and the candles were missing. Something told me to turn on the computer, and when I did, I realized it had been wiped clean. All my working files were gone!

In panic, I searched for my back-up storage devices, but they too were gone. My tablet—wiped clean. *All my life's work!* I thought as I accessed my smart phone, rushing the technology toward my cloud storage, only to find that it too was gone.

"Why? How? Dammit!" I screamed. "Sally!"

My first thoughts implicated her, but *why* would she do it? Why would she go out of her way to destroy my life's work? Surely, she understood how much my work meant to me. The content on those files and folders encompassed all my life's experience, all my thoughts—everything I have ever felt—every heartache, lesson, idea, concept, every breath and heartbeat. All my stories—gone, all my time with Mel—gone.

I could never get that back. She had deleted my entire life. Everything I had ever experienced was gone—it was as if my life had never happened. None of it was real. Without my work, I was nothing.

*****

I finally succumbed to tears, hoping Sally hadn't destroyed my back-up devices, hoping she had invaded my sacred zone merely to make a relationship point, to make me choose. I called her three times before I decided to drive to her house. When she opened the door, she greeted me with a smile and a passionate kiss.

"Are you okay? You don't look happy to see me."

"You were at my place last night," I huffed. "You were in my office. You destroyed all my work!"

"Let's sit down, have a glass of wine and talk about it," she insisted.

"Bullshit! I don't want to sit! I don't want your wine!" I shouted. "I want my work! Do you have my storage devices?"

"No. I'm sorry. They're gone, burned."

"You said you loved me, Sally! Why would you do that to me?"

"Let me explain," she said calmly. "It was difficult for me, but I did it for *us*. You don't understand now, but you will in time."

"You've ruined my life! You invaded my sacred space and destroyed my life. You did it for *you*! Why?"

"It's what you chose," she insisted.

"That's bullshit, Sally! You chose *for* me! How is that fair?"

"My purpose was not to destroy your work, but you left *me* no choice. It wasn't about your work. It was about her."

"Who?"

"Mel."

"Mel? What does Mel have to do with my work?"

"Everything. You said it yourself. Please understand. I didn't want to destroy your work. I wanted to shut down the channel and destroy the connection. You were incapable of doing it. Mel would have never let you go. *She's* the one who left you no choice. Please, dear heart, dear blood, sit down..."

I didn't want to sit. My mind was racing. It really *was* gone? *All my work!* How could I possibly go on? How could I ever write again, knowing what I had lost? I could never re-think those thoughts, re-tell those stories, re-imagine my life. As I slumped, she gently guided me toward the couch and forced me to sit.

"You can only love one of us. Your sacred writing space—it was your conduit to her, your *temple* to Melpomene. In order to destroy that clandestine, adulterous connection, I was forced to drag her altar down and burn your work, which bound your heart and soul to her, which was a product of your bond with her, your dissolute comingling with her! She claimed you and she would have never let you go, so that is why I had to destroy all pathways back to her. But in return, I've given you a treasure far more valuable than what you've lost."

"But my work! It's all gone!" I sighed. "You didn't let me choose to save my work! To save my life!"

"You chose the moment you decided not to run," she said. "I warned you. Now she'll never have a conduit to your life again."

"You had this planned all along. How did you do it? How did you figure out all my passwords? How did you find all my back-up storage devices—even the ones at my downtown office and my cloud back-ups—the hidden and encrypted ones?"

"We were together in your dream last night, and after making love, I asked about those things, and you shared all, so willingly. You knew what I would do. It was your way of letting go of Mel. Accept it now," she said and kissed my lips. "She's gone. You'll never see Melpomene again."

"How does it work?" I asked. "How do you visit me in dreams, and how do draugar 'swim through solid stone'?"

"In earnest, there is nothing magical about the things we do," she said. "From early on, my father and his researchers became intrigued with quantum physics, with a special focus on entanglement. They worked four hundred fifty years at our facility in Norway, and then finally, in 1925, our researchers developed the specific science that enabled us to teleport and to discover fluid time.

"In our experiments, we also took what humans understand as Schrödinger's Cat to previously unthinkable dimensions. Subject to limitation, we can literally be in two places at the same time. We're engineering divinity. We've built a tower that will reach the sky, a bridge between the physical and spirtual. And you don't want to be a part of that?"

"So all the things that draugar do is based on science and technology?"

"Throughout all history, technology and science amount to miracles and magic—even to *divinity*—within the eyes of humans who are ignorant.

"Now I feel trapped! You purposely set out to destroy my soul, Sally," I lamented, my heart sinking to the pit of my stomach, "because that's what you did when you took everything from me."

"Baby, I know what you're feeling right now," she whispered, taking my hands, peering into my eyes. "Anger, regret, ambivalence, confusion and hopelessness, but I promise you'll feel better. Soon, the petty work that Mel inspired won't matter because *we'll* have perpetual life together. *I* could be your Muse. Please take me in her place. You'll be able to do so much more with me. I'm authentic and I love you!"

"Love?" I sighed. "Maybe your sister was right. Is this what you do with all your victims? Is it all an act? She said you were a backstabber!"

"Please forgive me," she said, kissing me again, stroking my face. "Astrid was right about one thing: she tasted it in you. She guessed you were 98% compatible, but she didn't go far enough. You're closer to 99.8 %. It's why you were so attracted to me from the beginning and why there's such a connection between us—it's why we fell in love. We're nearly perfectly compatible."

"Ninety-nine-point-eight percent? What does that actually mean in draugar science?"

"It gives you a much better chance of surviving our comingling—maybe fifty percent. You have the rare prospect of perpetual life before you. The only risk now is you not wanting it enough, like Rai."

October 21 – The Golden Buddha

I noticed the statue again when I returned home that afternoon, placed in a position to the right of my front door. I had glimpsed it as I drove off that morning, wondering who had put it there, and then I remembered where I first saw it—it had always sat just to the right of Sally's front door. A gift? I noticed it was encrusted with mud when it was on her porch, so I thought I'd clean it up, but when I went to lift it, I strained and dropped it because it was so heavy.

I stepped back, confused. *How could an item so small be so heavy?* It was only eighteen inches tall, but it had to weigh over one hundred pounds. *It's as heavy as lead!* I thought, and then my eyes focused on an area of the seated figure where some of the crusted mud had been dislodged by the impact of the fall. It glistened gold, which suggested the statue had to be made of solid gold! I called Sally immediately and asked her to come over.

Before I left her condo on the previous afternoon, I told her I needed some time to sort my thoughts and grieve my work. I remained angry to the point of imagining revenge, but I believed her in my heart. Sally was probably right—I never would have given up Mel on my own.

I loved both, so I really was incapable of choosing. However, I resented the lack of closure. There was no final conversation with Mel, no goodbye, no period at the end of the sentence, no final page of our book. She simply was... gone.

I stayed awake on the couch that night so that Sally could not invade my dreams. I had gone to the space to meditate, seeking Mel, but I felt nothing. The connection was gone. I usually spent late nights writing when I could not sleep, but now I felt uninspired. There were no stories, no conversations playing in my head.

"I thought for sure I wouldn't see you today," Sally said, smiling. "You finally got over it? Losing all your writing?"

"No, I'll never be over it. That work went beyond my heart and soul. My *blood* was in that work."

"Then think of it as a blood sacrifice, a precursor," she said. "You invited me over for a *reason*?"

"Yes," I said, leading her out the front door. "Did you put *that* there?" I asked, pointing toward the Buddha.

"Yes," she said. "I brought it the night before last when I was with you. You didn't see it yesterday?"

"I was so distraught about my work that I wasn't seeing anything," I answered. "Why did you bring it here?"

"It's my gift to you, my own sacrifice in appreciation for the choice you made. It's 'Calling the Earth to Witness.' My father had it made in Thailand on the day that I was born. It's the single constant in my endless life."

I knelt, examining the statue more closely, noting the crossed legs, full-lotus posture, the left hand in the lap, the palm facing upward, and the right hand touching to the Earth with the palm facing inward. Sally explained its significance.

"This pose," she said, "represents the moment of enlightenment for Siddhartha and the very story of how, when he was at the verge of it, Mara, the Demon of Illusion, tried to dissuade him from taking the final last steps.

"Determined to suceed, Siddhartha meditated all night to overcome the fear and temptations sent against him, and when Mara and demonic followers demanded a witness, Siddhartha called the Earth Goddess to witness his realized enlightenment and share it with the world. Upon that, the Earth Goddess wrung her hair, releasing flood waters that swept the demon away. In that moment, Siddhartha became Buddha."

"Enlightenment," I responded, "I'm just struggling to understand what's happening to me. I never imagined realities beyond the parameters of humanity. I was certain I was aware and awake, but only now I realize the limitations of mortality and how little my short, pathetic life will let me understand."

"Enlightenment," she nodded. "And when we've comingled, you will see the world within a different light."

"And is that Buddha solid gold?" I asked. "It's so heavy."

"The body's 50% pure, the volume from the chin to the forehead is 90%, and the hair and the topknot are 99% pure gold. The statue was worth twenty-eight million dollars fifty years ago. You've lost your work, so I hope this Buddha's ample compensation."

"Wait!" I interrupted, "this crusty statue is worth millions of dollars, and you left it out on your porch? That's nuts!"

"I've had it my whole life and it's always been next to my front door. Humans are too superficial to understand what it is, while gold means little to draugar. Sell it if you want."

"No, I could never do that," I sighed. "I can't even accept it. You've had it your whole life. It must mean a lot to you."

"No more than your life's work meant to you. The root of suffering is attachment. The essence of The Way is detachment. In release, I free myself."

"Why would *I* sell it?" I asked. "I never wrote for financial profit."

"Then why did you write?"

"For the same reason that the salmon fights to swim up surging waterfalls. It's in my programming. It's impulse. I have no idea what I'm supposed to do when I get to the end of anything I write, and yet I always know it when it comes."

"You gonna leave the Golden Buddha on your porch?" she joked.

"That's exactly what I'll do," I replied. "The Earth is my Witness."

"One day you'll realize—this memory will save your life."

*****

We watched a movie that night—*Breakfast at Tiffany's*, our shared all-time favorite—Sally as vulnerable socialite Holly Golightly, and me as Paul Varjak, the smitten writer, ensnared in her dark web. There was a special moment in the film where the crucial conflict was in supreme focus.

In the final scene, Paul professes an attachment (a love) for Holly, who is determined to detach from all things, including her unnamed cat.

I don't want to own anything until I know I've found the place where me and things belong together. I'm not quite sure where that is just yet. But I know what it's like.

On the way to the airport, she puts the cat out of the car on a gloomy street in the pouring rain. In the story's resolution, Paul decides to live his truth and demands honesty from Holly. Finally facing reality, she overcomes her fear, and both are rewarded with love as they face an uncertain future. When they got there, they would know what to do.

"I've always loved this movie," she sniffed while wiping a tear. "It's so painfully... human."

"Me too," I sighed, batting back a tear, "nostalgically human. Look, if I comingle with you and I survive, how do you see perpetual life working out for us? I'd be a draugr. So next year, you'll have to find another human male to eat. What does that mean for us, when you've already insisted you don't date your draugar males. What happens then when there's another human male in love with you? Would you invade his dreams? And what if he survived?"

"Yet *after* you survive," she answered, "there'll be no other male attachment for me. You will be my sole perpetual partner, my counterpoint, and we will find divinity."

"But you will have to eat, and so will I. How will that work?"

"We'll go to Mothfest or figure something else out. We don't have to engineer the future. We'll just let it happen. We'll know."

"Mothfest? What's that?"

"It's coming up in LA next week," she answered. "We'll go. It'll be fun. I'm just excited about us."

"Why?"

"Because we're so compatible. I'm certain that once you become a draugr, we might even be able to have children. That's so huge!"

"Children? I don't understand."

"There hasn't been a draugr child born in one hundred fifty years, and researchers think the human survival rate from the blood exchange is shrinking. The window is closing—the survival rate is probably down to one percent. Humans and human blood are becoming less compatible for us. At some point, none will survive comingling."

"Which means nature has already slotted draugar for extinction," I concluded. "They just don't know it yet."

"We'll focus instead on getting you ready for the process," she said. "That'll be challenge enough, but I believe with all my soul that you're the one to The Way."

"I hope so."

"I'm going home so I can come to you tonight. You need to relax—don't fight me. When you're in the web, the female is the center of the universe. Trust me. Surrender your will, surrender choice."

October 22 – Divinity

"Do you believe in God?" I panted, out of breath, while testing how my feet were placed along the ledge and glancing down. I clutched the handholds tightly, hanging on.

"I am completely certain God exists," she answered, focusing while re-positioning her hips. Then Sally took an easy breath. "But am equally as certain he does not exist. It's just as matter can exist with anti-matter simultaneously, though not exclusively."

She easily pulled herself atop the summit ledge while steadying her feet, and reaching down, she grasped my hand and lifted me above the edge with little effort on her part.

"That being said," she then sustained, "there is a difference between believing God exists or yet believing 'in' Almighty God. For you, what does it mean to say that you believe 'in' God?"

I thought for a moment as I leaned forward, fingers gripping my thighs, catching my breath.

"I think it means acceptance and submission, rather than arrogance and rebellion."

She walked along the plateau to a small boulder formation, sat and swigged from her water bottle.

"Then more precisely, you should have asked me if I believed in 'God's *Purpose*.'"

"What is God's Purpose, according to you?" I asked, as I followed and plopped down next to her.

"God's Purpose is our *mission*, which is 'to know God's purpose.' It's why we exist—to pursue *knowing* it. I believe in Our Mission, which is indeed God's Purpose. So yes, you can count me a believer."

She raised her hand toward her face, examining the tiny creature crawling along her finger.

"Yet does it even live, if life is choice?"

"It serves a purpose. It's alive, and it can die," I said, "so it lives."

"Ants manifest the prodigy of God," she answered me, "to humble humans living on the Earth. Consider them, forever crawling everywhere, searching in quintillions, all individually irrelevant components, alive though not alive. Together, they transform themselves into a larger, more sophisticated organism, thus resembling the humans in their purpose on the Earth."

"But humans understand... we individually can have communion with our God."

"The concept of a God is inconceivable for humans who, like this female ant, will live a single season, wilt and die. So God is far beyond all human thought, imagination—let alone, all mortal comprehension—far beyond the things they understand. Thus it provides why humans, in their ignorance, should cease all efforts to conceive of God, this owing to an insufficient aptitude for knowing anything! They rather should endeavor understanding God's true *purpose* for humanity."

"What is God's purpose... for humans?" I asked.

"Consider first the tree professed possessing knowledge, good and bad. It was not necessary for the hearers of the cosmic enigmato know. The first two humans did not need to understand the heavenly-debated 'good and bad' to recognize and to achieve God's purpose, which was above all, to eschew the fruit belonging to the tree possessing knowledge, 'good and bad.'

"Examining our own creation allegory—our initial mother took—she touched the fatal fruit, and yet she did not eat of it. The sequel is the difference. On one hand, humankind is cursed to die, although eventually our Maitrix found the fated tree of life."

She held out her finger, allowing the ant's reintegration into the swarming tentacle on the rock where we sat.

"Do you believe that solitary ant could choose? And even if she could, the choice would be irrelevant and would not change a single thing. So could she really choose? But human choice is just as meaningless. They only *think* that they can choose, which makes the human only slightly better than the ant."

"Your ancient age has made you cynical," I joked, "when you compare a human to an ant."

"Yet can a single ant conceive that she is living in a nest beneath a rock upon a foothill on a plain within a continent upon a spherical globe within an orbit round a tiny star within a relatively unimportant galaxy within a massive swirling universe—a universe where only five percent of all existing matter can be measured, quantified and understood? The knowledge short-lived humans may possess is at the best one step up from the ant. The difference is irrelevant. An ant is unaware that it will die, but humans know that death is imminent."

"So perpetual life changes the essence of existence?"

"Yes, unavoidably. You'll never fully understand until it is your destiny, until you cease to live anticipating death, until you cease to be a slave to human-fabricated time. Humanity is but a thought of God, so humans are alive, while they are not alive unless awake. It's why both ants and humans can't conceive the will of God."

"And draugar can?"

"As you seek immortality, we seek divinity."

*****

I had picked Sally up at eight that morning, still exhausted after an enigmatic night of lucid dreams of us in the cottage, but we also visited a series of venues throughout time. I was myself, but I was also other people, as was Sally. *Residual engrams.*

We were in Mississippi on a slave plantation. During her visit with a friend in Natchez, we engaged in a forbidden love affair. She killed many humans to save me and took a profound risk in transporting me to Greenland, where she ultimately consumed me.

She later liberated an entire internment camp in Poland and ate me the next day. The violent/sensual dreams made even less sense after I awoke and saw the ring on the nightstand.

After breakfast at a café on the river, we drove up I-80 and then along US 49 until we reached Bowman Valley, nestled in a nook of the Nevada County portion of the Tahoe National Forest. The area afforded some of the most varied and high-quality rock climbing in the entire Sierra Nevada Mountain range.

Because we were on an advanced climb, I came equipped with a dynamic rope, a set of quickdraws, holds, a belay device and a climbing harness, while Sally, a freestyler, only brought climbing shoes.

*****

We had lunch and champagne overlooking the vast valley on that clear Monday afternoon. As far as we could see, we were alone at the top of the world—a rare perspective well-suited to our conversation.

"Isn't divinity 'being' God?" I asked.

"In a sense, *yes*," she answered, "but it's more about becoming *one* with God, to the point of transcending tangibility. God is the connection to and with all things—all matter in the universe. Authentic and omniscient ones become divine."

"And how does one become omniscient then?"

"The sole objective of omniscience is to know the language of divinity, thereby achieving unity with God."

"So are there wicked draugar?" I inquired.

"Not wicked, though some consciously resist achieving unity with God, and thus they seek their selfish motivations rather than God's purpose, though it's written in our hearts. Yet nowhere are they more distinguished from the rest than in their attitudes about divinity. Most wish to *be at one with* God—these draugar *love* divinity. But there're others who wish instead to *be like* God—thus *envying* divinity. Because they'll never be like God, their purpose is to guarantee no other draugar ever will."

And glancing from that lofty place, I looked upon two eagles, soaring high above the valley floor so far below us, causing me to reconsider what *transcendence* meant to me.

"How is it possible to break the bonds of tangibility?" I asked.

"While anticipating death, humans are not capable of understanding the relationship between tangibility and divinity," she said. "They can achieve enlightenment at best. Don't overthink it, sweetheart. When you are no longer human, your eyes will become open to all these things."

After another hour, we began our descent. Most free climbers used equipment on the trip down, but Sally scaled down the rockface with ease. While her unnatural weight caused some of the footholds to crumble above my head, she had the uncanny ability to quickly find replacements.

"You're only biologically immortal, so what would happen if you fell from here?"

"What do ya think would happen?" she laughed. "I'd go splat, just like you would! But I couldn't fall."

"Why couldn't you fall?"

"It goes back to our quantum mechanics technology, entanglement and fluid time," she answered. "Time binds us in the same way it binds humans, but we have discovered how to manage that fundamental quantity in dimensional analysis, which is equivalent to wiggle room, ranging more than half a minute, sometimes longer in emergencies. It's like being able to slip forward or backward in time fifteen to twenty seconds in the event of crisis or an accident."

"Which means you're living fifteen seconds, maybe even earlier, than humans on the Earth?"

"Typically, yes... or behind," she answered, "sometimes as a second look or instant replay. Think of your 'pause' on cable television—our technology is similar, though metaphysical. The way that we experience time is different."

"Oh, so you know what I am going to say at least fifteen or twenty seconds before I think to say it?"

"Most of the time, yes."

"But you *were* in an accident... with that truck!" I interrupted.

"That one happened too fast. I had just enough time to pulse phase between two places right at the moment of impact, making me temporarily intangible. Beyond that, I could have teleported if I could have done it in time."

"But you could have died if you hadn't seen it coming?"

"Still trying to figure out how to kill me?" she joked. "We can *always* see it coming... unless we're distracted, and I was definitely distracted that afternoon. Only a draugr could have done that."

"Can draugar kill other draugar?" I asked.

"That was no accident. It's possible for draugar to kill other draugar," she replied, concern showing on her face, "but it hasn't happened for over five hundred years. So in reality, we must contend with draugar wickedness."

October 23 – Astrid

"*Lequel préferez-vous, mademoiselle? La soupe ou la salade?*" the server asked, bowing as the train passed through the old industrial section of town, headed toward Yountville.

"*Je préfère la soup avec un verre de vin rouge, merci.*"

I picked Sally up at eight that morning, allowing two and a half hours driving time to reach Napa, locate the station and check in by 10:30. We got breakfast and coffee along the way.

The daytrip included a fifteen-minute seminar before boarding. As it turned out, I was able to buy the last two tickets for the excursion, which had been booked by a delegation of French tourists who had requested fluent French speakers as servers and guides.

Seated in a 1952 Pullman domed railcar with large windows, I wondered why there were two empty seats at our dining table. I couldn't imagine a couple not showing up after paying over six hundred dollars for the seats, but I was a little relieved because I didn't want company. I didn't like being at close quarters with strangers and feeling forced to engage in superficial conversation. I had Sally all to myself.

But it didn't surprise Sally when, twenty minutes into the trip, the missing couple showed up with champagne glasses, obviously intoxicated, dragging along a half-empty magnum of *Dom Perignon*. I hardly recognized the pale woman in the close-fitted red-silk dress, with flowing bright red hair and a blood-red manicure and pedicure—not until she spoke.

"*Bonjour! Bonjour, chère sœur, petite putain!*[7] *Quelle surprise! C'est incroyable, non?*" she laughed, kissing Sally once on each cheek. "*Quelle sont les chances!*[8]"

"You must have let her read your thoughts, *mon cher!*" an irritated Sally whispered in astonishment to me. "*Do not be weak with her again!*"

The clean-cut young man with Astrid couldn't have been older than twenty-five. He was roughly six-foot-three with a muscular build, a handsome face, a mass of thick dark-brown hair and ultra-white straight teeth.

"How did you know we were doing this today?" Sally asked in French. "This is my final warning: leave us alone or I will surely kill you."

"Dear sister," Astrid laughed, continuing in French "why all this talk of killing, when I am your favorite sister, your counterpoint? Whatever would you do without me?"

Astrid leaned over, kissing me once on each cheek.

"*Bonjour, petit garçon, mon petit oignon!*[9]" she smiled. "*Toujours avec ma sœur? Tu es fou!*[10]"

Placing the oversized bottle on the table, she motioned toward her date, indicating he should pull out her chair, and sat. He took the seat across from her, fixated, completely entranced by her, his hands all over her.

---

7 French — *little whore*
8 French — *What are the odds!*
9 French — *Hello, little boy, my little onion!*
10 French — *Still with my sister? You're nuts!*

"*Permettez-moi de présente mon déjeuner cet après-midi[11]*," she said before continuing in English. "This is Justin. He is a medical student at California University, Davis. He wants to be a surgeon, but why the need? He comes from old money. His great grandfather was a railroad baron from San Francisco. Justin—this is my younger sister, Sally... and her naïve little *boyfriend* for the month."

It was an uncomfortable moment that Astrid seemed to revel in. Sally was infuriated, though she struggled to hide it to deny her sister the satisfaction of triumph.

"It's very nice to meet you, Sally," Justin said. "You're very pretty, like your sister. I don't speak any French, but Anna said it wouldn't matter. I've never done anything like this before!"

"Poor boy," Sally responded. "You didn't realize that my sister was out of your league? What did you think she would want from *you*?"

"I don't know," he stuttered. "I'm going to be a doctor in a couple years... and I come from a respectable family."

"*Tais-toi, bonbon,*[12]" Astrid interrupted, her fingers to his lips. "I love Justin because he is so cute. Just look at those eyes—so soft and sensitive. This boy must love his mother."

"I do! I'm actually very close with my mother," he said. "She rocks!"

"*Je vais te manger,*" she cooed, stroking his cheek, flirting, almost singing. "*Je vais te manger.*"

"Okay, *whatever* she's saying," Justin said, ostensibly aroused, "it sounds totally sexy. I've gotta learn French."

"You won't, poor child. She said she is *going to eat you*," Sally translated. "You should run now, Justin. Jump off the train if you have to, little fool—you might break a few bones, but at least you won't be her lunch."

"Oh, I'd let *her* eat me!" he responded, seeming sexually excited. "I mean I can't *wait* to let her eat me."

"It's not what you're thinking," I chimed in. "Your life is in danger. She literally means to eat you."

---

[11] French – *Allow me to introduce my lunch for this afternoon.*

[12] French – *Shut-up, my sweet,*

"Don't I wish!" he said while leaning over to whisper to me. "You have no idea. She comes to me in my dreams, bro, and what she does is off the chains. She's such a tease!"

"*Et vous, mademoiselle? Lequel préféreriez-vous?*" the server asked Astrid.

"*Garder mon verre de champagne rempli. Je n'ai pas faim maintenant. J'ai déjà mon dejeuner.*[13]"

"*Monsieur?*" the server said to me.

"*Je préfère la soupe avec vin rouge et un apéritif aux crevettes.*[14]"

"*Et vous, monsieur?*" he said to Justin.

"*Wee, wee, gar-son,* he strained, grinning. "I'll have whatever he's having. I trust you, bro."

The five-course lunch was exquisite. Sally had the butternut squash gnocchi, while Justin and I opted for the halibut. Astrid had only champagne.

The four of us swirled cognac as we waited to depart for the Motorcoach that would spirit us to *Castello di Amorosa*, an authentically-styled 13th century castle, complete with a moat, grand halls with hand-painted walls, wine cellars and an historic torture chamber and armory.

I felt sorry for Justin, so I pulled the young man aside to whisper a stern warning.

"She's not what you think she is, Justin. Don't let her get you alone. She's really going to eat you!"

"I'm feelin it, bro," he nodded. "She's totally hot!"

"I'm feelin you, but *bros before hoes*—know what I'm sayin?" and then I whispered. "*She going to kill you!*"

It was useless. He was entirely taken by her, as if under a spell, like the man in the bar, like the moth unto the flame. Glancing over at her, I conceded for the first time that Astrid was extraordinarily attractive, though not in the authentic way that Sally was.

---

[13] French – *See to it that my champagne glass remains filled. I'm not hungry now. I already have my lunch.*

[14] French – *I prefer the soup with red wine and a shrimp appetizer.*

She had a more primitive, carnal and naughty quality that was captivating, though profoundly more coquettish. I resisted as Astrid approached, trying to bring poor Justin to his senses.

"Are you a human, Anna?"

"Hell-to-the-*No!*" she answered, smiling. "I hate humans."

Justin only shrugged. "Yeah, I get it. Humans suck!"

"How old are you?" I asked, continuing.

"Hey dude—stop blockin. I don't care," he interrupted, "look at that bangin body! I'll eat *her*. I'm gonna tear that up! That's what *I'm* talkin bout!" he said while groping her.

"*Quel idiot! Regarde moi,*[15]" she said to me before turning back to the aspiring medical student. "I'm eight-hundred-ninety-two-bitchin-years-young! I'm a force of nature."

"Eight-hundred-ninety-two!" I crowed. "She's telling you the truth! You're gonna die."

"I love older women," he answered, eyes glazed as she flirted. "I'm sure she could teach me a few things!"

"Tell him what you are, Anna."

"I'm Draugar, and I eat human males because they're assholes and I love to watch them die, and right now, I want to have a promising future doctor for lunch in the torture chamber. A human, you're too ignorant to understand, but I'm *really* going to eat you, Justin."

"Awesome!" he exclaimed, his hand grabbing her ass.

Sally turned me toward her before I could argue further.

"It's no use," she sighed. "Moth to the flame. *Il ne peut s'aider.*[16]"

When I turned back to Justin, he and Astrid were gone. Sally explained she had probably teleported him to a secluded place where she could eat him in private.

*****

"She wore the red dress and red wig so that his blood won't show."

---

[15] French – *What an idiot! Watch this.*
[16] French – *He can't help himself.*

"What will she do with the body?" I asked.

"She'll teleport it to a secret crypt. My guess—behind a wall or bulkhead, since this is a castle, or somewhere far away. Astrid's always been clever about hiding bodies."

Astrid was absent for most of the castle tour. When she rejoined Sally and me during the wine tasting, a drop of blood still lingered at the corner of her mouth and her face was flushed—she had the appearance of a post-orgasmic woman. She licked her lips, savoring the flavor, winking at me.

Wary of her older sister, Sally kept her own body between mine and Astrid's at all times. I heeded Sally's oxytocin warning about physical contact, avoided eye contact and kept my distance, but during the Motorcoach ride back to Napa, I faced the dilemma of either sitting next to Astrid or across from her. As Sally sat next to her, I fixed my gaze into my girlfriend's eyes.

"*Ooh, J'adore bien le Gormánuður!*"[17] Astrid sighed while seductively crossing a shapely leg and twirling her ankle, dangling a wispy, lacy red velvet Louboutin stiletto. "Are we speaking in English now? I absolutely love Gormánuður! Did Sally tell you what that is, you handsome little boy?"

"I mentioned it to him. It's Slaughter Month, beginning on your October 14th," Sally explained. "During this month, the ancients celebrated the harvest by slaughtering animals to store up for the winter. Nowadays, it's the month in which omniscient-minded draugar return to Greenland for *Seiðr*."

"I take it Astrid doesn't attend the event?"

"I don't for myriad reasons," Astrid huffed, irritated, "the first of which is its tacit endorsement of draugar subjugation by humans. I despise humans and the male-dominated, testosterone-driven, sexist world they've created that exploits, demeans and murders females of all species! They're so proud of themselves, while they're so ignorant. If they weren't necessary, I'd butcher every last human, but for now, I'll just enjoy slaughtering their arrogant and perverted males."

"Do you hate human *females*, Astrid? I countered then.

---

[17] French – Oh, *I really love Gormánuður!*

"I do," she said, "because they are the ones who birth the horrid human males!"

"Do you privately hate humans as well, Sally?" I asked.

"Hate is a subtle word when it comes to humans," she shrugged. "They are ignorant and annoying, especially the males, who mostly I resent. There have been times when, like my sister, I've felt a certain sense of pleasure at the sight of an arrogant human male in misery, but no, I don't hate humans in the same way that she does."

"Pathetic humans have no right to rule in place of draugar, who are their betters!" Astrid sighed. "Damn all human males to death!" she loud declared and then she smiled.

"*Ah, excusez-moi!* We must remember Justin now, another idiotic human male..." She took a nearly-full wine bottle from her purse, which she uncorked and poured it into one of the four clean glasses on the limo bar between us. Glancing toward Sally, she poured a second and then a third glass. "*Vin sanglant?*"

I understood immediately what was in the glass before me. Only half the dark crimson liquid was wine.

"That's really Justin's blood?"

"To Justin's memory. *Salut!*" she said and sipped. "*Mmm, ooh-la-la!* So fresh... and it's still warm," she sighed and drank again. "*Umami! Très formidable!* The cabernet varietals are so excellent for *le vin sanglant*,[18] *n'est-ce pas? Chère sœur...*"

She took the second glass from the bar and offered it to Sally.

"Do not pretend to be so coy, dear sister. How many nights have we drank to intoxication *le vin sanglant*? Come, come, dear sister—it's Gormánuður. You know you love it. Certainly, you remember last year, and you no doubt remember our Rai!"

"No *vin sanglant* today. I have no appetite for wine with you!"

"*Rabat-joie!*[19]" Astrid tisked, turning toward me. "What about you, my sister's sexy, tempting boyfriend and a would-be draugr? Have but one sip—a taste of immortality!"

---

[18] French – *bloody wine*
[19] French – *Killjoy!*

I could neither answer nor look in her direction. I wasn't going to drink Justin's blood.

"So innocent and so obedient," she sneered, glaring toward Sally, taunting her. "Я собираюсь съесть твоего маленького бойфренда."[20]

"*Du er forbi din tid, gamle kvinne. Hvis du rører ham, vil du dø!*"[21] Sally responded in anger.

I had no idea what they said in the exchange, which definitely wasn't French. Astrid's words sounded Russian, while Sally's response seemed remotely German or Scandinavian. Whatever was said raised the tension level in the car. The sisters appeared to be evenly-matched, physically, and both possessed draugar technology for teleportation, phasing, fluid time and who knew what else. Astrid was cruel, while Sally was cunning.

I feared being trapped between those two forces of nature if Sally lost her temper, but her two-hundred-ninety-odd-years of experience, immortality and the pursuit of divinity had taught her self-discipline and patience. She shielded me from Astrid's glower until we got back to the Napa train station.

It was frightening to know that without Sally's protection, her sister would have eaten me with a sadistic relish. Once outside the car, the sisters hugged and kissed, offering insincere pleasantries. While hugging me, Astrid whispered quietly into my ear.

"*Et iterum autem videbo vos cito,*" which I understood, having studied Latin in my youth. She had chanted into my ear, singing, "*I will see you again soon.*"

October 24 – System Restore

When Mel returned, I was not asleep, but neither was I awake. I was in the realm of visions, the place where perhaps Noah received divine foreknowledge and instruction, where A'bram, through God's divination, received the promise of human redemption, where Zaphnath-Paaneah and Belteshazzar gained the insight to understand the language of divinity.

---

[20] Russian — *I'm going to eat your little boyfriend.*
[21] Norwegian —*You're past your time, old woman. If you touch him, you will die!*

I thought I heard her whispering during the morning and fancied she was sitting next to me in the afternoon as I sat at my computer. I was even able to set my thoughts across the digital transverse.

I watched as she traversed the room and sat across from me. Her beauty was not earthly, but something more intricate—perfection, extending to every hair on her head, to every cell of her body. Yet rather than desire, her exquisiteness inspired admiration then... and even worship in my heart. She placed her hands atop my own.

"Why have you taken leave of me?" she asked, this while she seemed exceedingly concerned.

"I didn't leave you," I answered. "You remember Sally? She is the draugar female who you saw who came to visit me? She said she loved me and demanded that I choose between herself and you. She came into my office and my life to purposely destroy the work that we created in this space. It's gone—our every story, file, idea and inspiration—all the hours that we spent in our communion and collaboration. It's all gone. She destroyed our connection!"

"Am I a new acquaintance in your life?" Mel mocked, *"who has not sat beside you as a seeming wife so many years? And am I not divine? Do you believe a silly corporal upstart could supplant my will? She has the modest learning of three hundred years—the wisdom of a child—when I possess a knowledge that exceeds eternal mortal age."*

"I've tried to write since then," I frustratedly complained, "but I can't write if you are not beside me. Now my work is gone. All the erstwhile words I've written haunt me now, inspiring only grief and then regret for what is lost forever, so I am demoralized. I thought that I would never hear your voice again."

"You will enjoy my inspiration once again," she said. *"Our work is not undone or gone. We can restore our every word and syllable."*

"How is that possible?" I asked.

"My intervention is divine," she said. *"I knew the thinking of that silly little girl before she even knew to think of it. Before she*

violated our sacred space to devastate your work, your Muse directed you in sleep to generate a second, back-up drive, a secret source your conscious mind would not remember—no, not till I reminded you."

"Reminded me of what?" I asked. Then I remembered what was lost to me. One evening as I sat within my mid-town office in creative stupor, I felt compelled to rise up from the desk and to perform a task that I immediately forgot once I completed it!

It was a series of procedures I'd repeated numerous times, but on that night, it seemed that someone else controlled my mind and hands. Yes, then it seemed that I remembered dreaming that I'd backed up all my work on an external drive and mailed it to an address unfamiliar to my memory, some foreign address that I did not know.

*****

"*This foolish girl is not to be believed or loved,*" Mel said. "*Love is divine. You cannot love her, neither does not she love you as I do. She is a simple, creeping, crawling carnal creature made for copulation, yet without capacity for love. 'Down from the waist, she is a Centaur, yet a woman all above.'*

"*Her female charms have stirred the inner nature you've suppressed till now. She has enticed with flesh and intellectual device to overcome your will and common sense. So you have been ensnared, have stumbled foolishly into her web.*"

"Where were you, Mel?" I asked. "Where have you been? How did you, my Muse and my protector, let this happen to your voice?"

"*The fault is yours for your unfaithfulness,*" she said, "*the treachery of your lusting heart. Have I not given all that you have asked of me? She came into your bed, and you did not reject her overtures. You readily defiled the vows that bonded us. The sequel is the consequence.*"

"But I was overwhelmed," I answered her. "I am an ordinary man against a force of nature! I never stood a chance. What is the consequence? Are we undone?"

"*By now you realize that your creative soul belongs to me,*" she said, "*you are indeed my voice, so you must choose to have a mate who is divine and must reject a match of draugar flesh.?*"

"I cannot lose my Muse again, but what am I to do? And how might I authenticate my choice?" I asked.

"*Before all else,*" she said, "*you must return the Golden Buddha to her home. If she refuses it, then cast it down into a watery abyss where it will not be found. She uses it to overwhelm your will, to make you prey to her, to make you offer sacrifice.*"

"If I no longer have the Golden Buddha at my door," I asked, "what must I do to have my work restored? What must I do to have you next to me again?"

"*You must reject this silly girl and all she offers you. She lies to proffer immortality, when all she wants is to devour you, to steal your blood, your vital energy and will. Reject her, then restore your sacred writing space, but never see or speak with her again. Repel her if she comes at night, and do not let your mind remember her. She is a test of character, and when you prove your worth, your life and work will be restored, and I will come again to you.*"

"But Sally said she offered choice, which left no choice at all. Is it the same with you?"

"*You have no choice because the choice was made for you. You'll never understand, but not because you are incapable. If she could truly grant you immortality, then over time you'd understand where humans erred. There is one choice, and only one—the rest of mortal life is exercise.*"

"What is that choice?" I asked.

"*The choice of 'good and bad'—not 'good or bad.' Within the riddle of the trees, do not forget there were TWO trees: the tree that offered knowledge and whose branches offered fruit, both good and bad—and then there was the tree that offered immortality.*

"*The fruit of knowledge offered fleshly choice, while yet the fruit of life eternal offered heavenly omniscience, where there is no choice. The human female chose which tree from which to pick and eat and share, but she was immature, without capacity to differentiate between the two. The fruit was choice itself. She chose for humankind, and so her seed must live the consequence. The end result is all the same. No matter what they think that they can choose, all humans die. Inconsequential choice is not free-will at all."*

*****

"What do you know of draugar?" then I asked. "Can they attain divinity?"

"One hundred fifteen billion beings have been born on Earth as flesh and blood and bone, yet only nine have gained divinity. The rest will fare no better than the humans seeking immortality. It is the ancient story of the spider and the ant, another riddle in the language of divinity. Which crawling creature is superior? Which do you think you are?"

"The single spider is superior in every way," I answered her, "much stronger and more cunning than an ant alone."

"And yet against a colony of ants, the spider is no match. The spider sees no profit in cooperation, since the spider is a singularity, while ants surrender individuality and will for order, program and design—their genius lies in connectivity. In shortened form, the draugr is the spider and the human is the ant. A single spider is a force of nature, while an ant alone is but a morsel in her web. The draugr preys on humankind, though secretly, she fears humanity."

Mel's flawless face began to glow as there she sat across from me with piercing, mesmerizing eyes, and yet unfaithful proved my heart, at once becoming stirred with thought. Mel had insisted Sally did not love me, yet within my heart I knew that what I felt was more than something of a physical, instinctual, and an ill-advised connection that she called a 'consequence of fate.'

I knew it from the moment that I first held Sally's naked body close against my own and felt her racing heart. She held me tight and whispered words into my ear. *I love you!*

"How many others has she held and spoke those words?" Mel said, while she seemed to read my heart and mind. *"How many has she loved before today? Perhaps three hundred men?*

Or yet five hundred men? One thousand? You are a novelty to her, a rare and aged libation, meant for savoring."

"Then what am I to you?" I asked. "I know I'm not the only poet you've possessed or whispered to. How many others over time? Perhaps ten thousand? So what benefit am I to you?"

"You are my Seventh Scribe, my final instrument, as there will never come another after you—my sacred voice, to write the words Melpomene woud speak unto all time, while in exchange, I grant you wisdom and the lyric gift, but you may never love a fleshly female in your life, must never take another mate."

****

"So is it true that she has lied to me?" I asked. "Have draugar truly mastered immortality?"

"They have the coveted eternal spark, which humans lost in their demise."

"This draugr, Sally, says that we are perfectly compatible, that I can live forever at her side. Is that a lie?"

"That is the fabricated sheen of light upon her web. When viewed just right in subtle rays of sun, it hides and transforms its design to guarantee that you are firmly caught. I've watched it happen many times to moths and men. She's chosen you."

"She is a singularity," I said, "so she could choose a king or prince or any other man. Why has she chosen me?"

"She will not tell you, but there's something else she sees in you that I have seen since first you were conceived. She's watched and waited countless years and did not recognize it once before this year. Your perspicacious and presumptuous draugr sees it only now. Be warned: your meeting was no accident. She sought you out and found you for a selfish opportunity."

"But I'm an ordinary human male," I insisted while confused. "What could she want from me?"

"The draugar have the spark for life in perpetuity, their coveted 'eternal spark.' But she has found the Radical—the rumored, legendary singularity that they have sought throughout their history. I see it glowing in you even now. The

spark that you possess is something rare. You have the spark that promises divinity!"

"What does that mean?" I begged. "I do not understand."

"She saw the spark in you and knew that you could help her and her kind to gain divinity, and that is why she sought to sever the spiritual connection that we've shared. She lied to you to win your gift. She has not told you everything."

"What of this spark?" I asked.

"The spark is not divinity itself. Instead, it is a gift—a rare potential for divinity, if understood. A hybrid possibility. The irony however, is that humans die too soon to ever understand. I see her thoughts: if she can help you gain eternal life, then you can help her to attain divinity."

"So tell me, honestly," I pleaded then, "you've given me the opportunity to taste and savor—even bask in winds of love divine, though they do not contain the faintest whisper of divinity. What should I do?"

"Return the Golden Buddha. Never entertain that scheming whore again," she answered me. *"I am your mate in this dimension till you die. You know what you must do. Return to me, and I'll return to you!"*

October 25 – Draugary

For hours after Mel had left, I sat and contemplated my relationship with Sally, reflecting on the day we met, three weeks earlier. She seemed so virtuous and innocent... and even vulnerable. *To think that she was not a human female all along!* I remembered meeting then her father and our initial date with questions and response. *Run now!* she said ironically, *run now before you know!* I was so overcome by her intrigue and beauty that, in irony, I did not hear or comprehend her words.

I was no better off than Justin, who could not imagine or believe Astrid's intent, this even after she had said outright that *I'm going to eat you now!*

How was I any different? When all was said and done, would I mean any more to Sally than the foolish Justin meant to arrogant Astrid? Was Sally *really* different than her sister was?

And over time, how many men like me had Sally lured into her silken chamber on October thirty-first, specifically to pleasure and devour them in Gormánuður, or Slaughter Month.

She said that she loved Rai, but where was he? And going forth one year in time, would I be nothing more than him, a cherished memory, a morsel, worthy of a tear occasionally? Why did I love? Why did she make me care? At least Astrid was honest, yet it did not make a difference. The sad result would always be the same, except for love.

I too deplored the way that Sally toyed with my affections, dragged my heart to do what it had never done. I never loved a fleshly female in the vain, besotted way that I loved Sally—to the point of self-imposing immolation. If she truly loved me, then she never would have let me fall in love with her. Though to her credit, she had warned me off, although I didn't listen. My warning to all human males: *beware of seeming seemly women overfriendly in October—only if you wish to live.*

I got the sense that Sally still was hiding something from me, making me suspicious and aloof. That and the fact that she had violated my own consecrated space specifically to sever my connection to my Muse, to Mel. She knew that it would be the end of all my work and all it meant to me.

Why hadn't Sally chosen someone else with less to lose? Perhaps Astrid was right? and Mel as well? Was Sally's calculated conduct in our last three weeks a necessary predator's deception, a spider's calculated web?

*****

I still remembered Sally's face that night Astrid held out *le vin sanglant*, composed of cabernet varietals and Justin's blood. Her mouth was watering. I knew she craved to drink until she saw the horrorstruck expression on my face. Almost three hundred years! How many men professed their love to her? How many had she loved and ate them afterward.

She swore that I was different, and nearly perfectly compatible, that we could live as lovers for eternity. But hadn't she professed the same to Rai?

I sat there in the dark, remembering her kisses and the moment she confessed her love to me. I closed my eyes and I imagined Sally in my arms, inhaling to evoke the female essence of her skin. And as I heaved my chest, then I could feel her heartbeat, close to mine. I sighed, revisiting the dreams in which she came to me, the sensual way our bodies danced, the deep connection we experienced, but all those things were destined for the past, were things I'd soon forget.

Yes, I decided that I'd run from her to save my life. By then I was convinced that draugar were a cruel, efficient, predatory race, that I was nothing more than prey.

It seemed that Mel had told me how to struggle free from Sally's web, and it involved the Golden Buddha she had placed beside my entryway. *Return the wicked, evil statue to her door,"* Mel said, *"for only then will you escape that awful whore.* And that's how I'd be rid of her!

I stayed away from my apartment the entire day, avoiding her, and I returned a little after nine p.m. I did not enter. On the porch, I strained to lift the Golden Buddha from its place beside my door and struggled hard to carry it and load it in my Jeep.

While nervous all along the way, I drove and I approached her condo, watching timidly and creeping in the vehicle along the curb in front of where she lived. Then quiet, careful, I removed the statue from the Jeep and carried it to that vacated space beside her door and plopped it down.

As I stood listening, I heard a sad and somber song profusing from her stereo inside. Emotions wrought, I thought to peek into the window for a final look at her, but I remembered—still could hear Mel's warning in my ears. Regretting as I drove away, I painfully resolved that I would never see her face again.

Of all the females I had ever known, this Sally seemed the most authentic person I had ever met, and when she said at last she loved me, I believed with all my heart that she was speaking honestly, that she was telling me her truth.

*****

I was exhausted when I got back to my place, but I was so distraught about the choice I made that it was hard to fall asleep. Within the last two weeks, it seemed I had acquired an addiction to the *Akvavit* that Sally had provided, as my tortured conscience longed for restful sleep that it induced. I sipped two shots before I stumbled to my bed.

The cottage seemed the same, but it was different, a smaller area, I thought, an older feel, perhaps. The bed was not as I remembered it. The fireplace was not as large and did not fully light the room. I was in the bed, beneath the quilts and reindeer fur, unclothed. The goblet filled with Akvavit was just beyond my reach. Unlike before, I felt intoxicated lying there, and then I realized that I was not alone.

She seemed upset with me, much more aggressive than she was before, which made me balk and move away from her. Yet she pursued relentlessly with force and will, though I resisted, realizing there was something out of synch. Her spirit did not feel the same, as I sensed cruelty and spitefulness I never felt before, and all because I had rejected her, returned the Golden Buddha to its place beside her door. And finally, I saw her for the draugr that she was—a calculating female beast, incapable of love.

With all my will I fought to drive her from the bed, which with great difficulty I was able to achieve. Then suddenly, I was alone with nothing but my thinking and my fear. I was confused, since Mel herself had told me what to do and how I might escape the draugar in my dreams, so I was not prepared for her return.

This time she wanted something different, and gentler than before, she soft caressed my face and gently kissed my lips, preparing for a more substantial interchange. As I began to yield, I felt a sense that something still was inappropriate, so I began to fight again.

She tried to force herself on me. We fought a war of wills for hours lying there, and finally I was alone again. I felt a sense of vindication, mollified my guilt toward her, and finally, I understood I had at last escaped her web.

Yet once again, I had no memory of the dream until an hour after I awoke, the ring as the reminder—yet not by Sally's runic ring. There was another ring there in its place. It was a ring I knew I'd seen before, though I did not recall distinctly where.

October 26 – Compulsion

For over twenty-four hours I had ignored Sally's calls. It was difficult, but Mel said it was the only way for me to restore myself and return to my work. I tried to convince myself otherwise, but I still loved Sally—perhaps more than ever. I was just worried that she didn't love me, that our relationship ultimately required her to use me up.

As the end of the month loomed closer, I knew the time would come for her to consume me. She would expect it, and I would be helpless to resist. In the end, I thought the better prospect was for me to get back to my work and pretend I had never met her.

Head bowed as I sat at the foot of my bed, the dream from hours earlier bothered me even more. Why was Sally so angry and violent with me? Was she finally showing me her true self, her cruel side, which reminded me of her sister? I remembered one of our conversations when she told me she would release me from any obligation to her if I changed my mind and didn't want to share the risk of an eternal relationship with her. Was that another one of many lies she told?

The ring on the nightstand confused me. I had never seen her wear it before. The design seemed more Middle-Eastern, possibly Egyptian. Though the dream was detailed and precise when it returned to me, it quickly faded like a mist so that I struggled to remember anything at all.

*****

I held the ring in my hand to remind me, and I was studying it in detail when I heard the knock at my door.

"Where have you been, you idiotic male?" she asked. "Why haven't you been answering my calls?"

"Because I decided I couldn't go through with it," I said. "I love you, Sally, but you're asking me to risk my life with the odds of success being one in one hundred—which means I'll probably be dead in a week and you'll be fine and energized. You're risking nothing, while I'm risking everything."

"I understand that," she said, still outside, "but how can you say you love me and treat me this way? You just go into hiding and refuse to communicate with me at all? Didn't I already tell you that I wouldn't have ill feelings or resent you if you changed your mind?"

"Yes."

"But you didn't believe me," she sighed as tears began to form in her eyes. "And why did you secretly return the Golden Buddha I gave you as a gift? And what's this by your door?"

Stepping outside, I glanced down to the right of my front door to see another golden statue, this one in the form of the Egyptian Isis—one knee on the ground, one knee raised, with outstretched wings and intricately-designed, iridescent feathers.

"What is that?" I asked, confused.

"It's my sister's statue! It's Astrid's!" she blurted, batting back tears. "How could you? You swore you loved me!"

"No!" I protested, accidentally dropping the ring. "I thought *you* came to me. I didn't know that it was her!"

"Astrid! That is her ring. You shunned me and avoided me to be with *her*?"

"Please, Sally—that is not the truth! I swear!"

"That statue is her claim to you. As long as it is at your door, I'm barred from teleporting in or using draugar science and technology while I'm here. It severs all our history and our hopes."

Scrambling to retrieve the ring, I looked more closely at the statue, realizing who had come to me within the night. It wasn't Sally in my dream—Astrid had somehow crawled into my bed!

"I'm sorry, Sally! Please, I want to talk to you. I will remove your sister's statue from my door. I'll dump it in a lake not far from here. I'll do that now, and then I'll meet you at the coffee shop. So if you really love me, you'll be there!"

*****

She was waiting at our window table when I arrived at the coffee shop, but she did not seem happy to see me.

"Why did you return the Golden Buddha to my door? And who demanded that you to do this thing?"

"It wasn't your sister," I protested. "It was Mel."

"Mel?" she sighed. "But that's impossible."

"No, it isn't. She's divine. Mel did return to me, and in her cryptic words, she told me that you'd never let me go. She said you only wanted me for some prophetic spark that grants divinity. She indicated that the only way to save myself would be removing your enchantment over me, and she directed me to move the Golden Buddha from my porch, return the statue to your door."

"You think the female who you saw was Mel?" she asked. "I pulled her altars down and severed your connection to her false divinity! That female wasn't Mel. It was Astrid, disguised to seem like Mel! She must have found a way into your home!"

"No, it was Mel. I'm sure of it," I said, "since no one else would know to say the things she did that night. I tell you it was not Astrid. You failed to censure her. She found a way back in."

"You are a fool to think it otherwise!" then Sally said. "Why can't you see the truth? It was Astrid! Mel's dead to you."

"No, it was Mel," I argued ardently. "You obviously did not destroy the link we share. When you and I first met, Mel surreptitiously influenced me to make a secret back-up of my work, which cleverly she hid from me, all purposed to protect me from your treachery."

"She told you to return the statue to my door? But why would Mel do that?

"She did, and so I did," I answered her.

"So that is how Astrid got in!" then Sally snarled and fumed. "She must have been a witness to your words with Mel. And when she saw my statue gone, she went right in. And you succumbed to her—like Rai succumbed!"

"No!" I protested, "I did not succumb. She came to me while I was in my bed. That much is true. At first, I thought that it was you and you were angry, but I sensed that she felt different than you do. I know you love me—I could feel the difference, so I fought her. I fought all night with all my might, but I did *not* succumb to her!"

"That's good," she smiled. "You said you *felt* the difference? Well, now you see that Mel was wrong concerning me. So will you always doubt my love for you? And do you now have faith that I would free you if you truly wanted to be free?"

"Yes, I believe you love me, but you have not told me everything I need to know to be informed when I decide. What do you know about a spark, about a Radical, a *hybrid* possibility, one which involves divinity?"

"I've sought divinity for my entire life," she said. "There are not ample draugar in existence now to hope that it would randomly occur within our population, but because there are so many humans on the Earth, we knew it would occur in various predicted intervals.

"Statistically, the number who possess the spark cannot be measured, though our scientists developed a predictive software app, allowing us to measure traces of a DNA divinity potential in specific human populations. Your Muse, Melpomene, was right. You have the spark."

"What does that mean to you?"

"It means that once you are immortal, we can then become divine, if that is what *you* want."

"So was our meeting accidental? Did you seek me out?"

"I did not seek you out specifically, but I'm a draugar scientist. Statistically, I knew the time was right, and you existed somewhere in this given area, so I came to find the Radical. Because I knew that we would be so overpoweringly compatible and knew that you'd be drawn to me like moth to flame, I only had to wait. I knew that over time that you'd abandon your good senses and you'd hurl heart and mind into my web. In truth, we sought each *other* out."

"But why warn me to run?" I asked.

"Because I knew that you'd be stubborn and tenacious and would do the opposite, entangling yourself. Your male compulsion drives behavior that's predictable, so in the end, you had no choice. But you've succeeded where so many others failed."

*****

"What about Rai?"

"That gentle man succumbed to all my sister's lures and charms, but in the end, I knew it was because he always had a crush on her. Astrid's seductions render males effete and powerless, and females too."

"What did she do?" I asked.

"Rai let her do exactly what she wanted. Then she ate my boyfriend, draining every drop, a Class IV hemmorage."

"So if it was not Rai in last October, who exactly did you eat?"

"I had to eat an ordinary and disgusting human male—which made my stomach sick for several months," she finally replied. "Tomorrow's Saturday. I mentioned Mothfest, didn't I? I said we'd go to Mothfest in Los Angeles. Tomorrow night, we'll go."

"Wait! You didn't tell me what it was."

"Well, it's a place where many draugar go to find someone compatible. And it's a place where we are not required to disguise our predatory nature. We can be authentic there, as flames for all the desperate moths, unlike pathetic, clumsy human females there who spin such obvious flimsy webs. So many in attendance come as eager sacrificial lambs for us, and even those who know the odds."

"Wow! Why haven't I heard about it? Mothfest?" I asked.

"I'm sure you have. You know it by a different name. Astrid will be there, and I'm sure that after you rejected her, she'll be on one big *rager* there. I pity all the men she'll catch within her web tomorrow night!"

Sally tossed four half-inch circular metallic discs onto the table. "Your transportation for the night."

"What are those?" I asked.

"Teleportation implants. Beats the five-hour drive and the TSA process at the airport. Once they're implanted in you, we can get there within a fraction of a second. That way, we won't wait in line, go through security or pay the entry fee."

*****

Sally and I had dinner that night at her condo after she surgically implanted discs in me for teleportation and for phasing. After programming an advanced, invisible-to-the-naked-eye, plc-based micro-control panel implant on my left wrist, she performed several diagnostic tests to assure the system was on-line and working.

While she tried to demonstrate how it would work, I was content to copy actions that she took when it was time to phase and teleport. I hurled three times until the dinner I ate was gone.

"I sorry for today and what I did," I said, wiping my mouth. "I sure remember how I felt when you avoided me. I should have called you, and I should have been confident enough to share my insecurities."

"No harm, no foul," she smiled. "At least you're alive. On this day last year, I lost my boyfriend to my sister's lust-filled appetite, so as I told you, I attended Seiðr with an ordinary, generic human male. Tomorrow night, you must avoid my sister at all costs. She's desperate for your blood."

"Do you love me?" I asked.

"Enough to risk my own eternity so we might gain divinity," she answered me.

October 27 – Mothfest

When I got home, the Golden Buddha was again beside my door, and Sally came to me within my dreams. I don't remember doing any more than cuddling, and she was gone. I saw the runic ring upon the nightstand when I woke and cupped it to my heart, inhaling deeply from the sweet and gentle fragrance in her wake. I winced in fear, at once remembering Astrid was with me in my bed one night before. I didn't understand how I survived. Perhaps it was the presence of Melpomene.

Mel had demanded I should never see my kindred draugr soul again, but since she was omniscient and divine, she must have known that Sally's absence would deliver other blood-consuming creatures to my bed, especially if it was known to them I held the prospect of divinity. She must have known that Sally would return. I didn't know what Mel had planned for me, since I could not begin to comprehend divinity.

*****

Mothfest—both Sally and Astrid called it that, but I had never heard of it. All I knew was that it was in Los Angeles and it was supposed to be some draugar smorgasbord. I also knew that Sally and I would be phasing and then teleporting down there. As she explained it, "phasing" was the entanglement technology where a draugr could appear to be in two places at one time, although she actually was in either one place or the other. Phasing allowed a draugr to bounce back and forth between two places at such a high frequency that to the naked eye and in reality, the draugr was in both. The process, however, required an enormous amount of energy.

Phasing was necessary for teleportation since the draugr teleporting needed a precise target location. By phasing, a draugr could bounce back and forth from a specific present location to a general target location. While in the target location, the draugr could eventually position herself into a precise target location and commence the teleport. It sounded complicated, but Sally's only concern was my structural integrity, since draugar were fifteen percent denser than humans. She said I was at least nine percent denser, which was the minimum requirement for teleportation and phasing.

Sally also installed an implant attached directly to my cochlear, or auditory nerve. The device allowed direct communication between draugar who activated the "send and receive" feature on the wrist implant control panel.

During active mode, a draugr could choose to communicate with another draugr by simply thinking words and listening. Sally said that it would take me perhaps a few months to master the ability for creating words and fluid sentences, but I would be able to hear and understand her communications and those of other draugar who spoke directly to me.

*****

"*Are you ready?*" she asked. "*I'm not gonna take my truck to your place.*"

I heard her voice as clearly as if she was in the room. I tried to form the words to answer, but my responding was beyond impossible. I wondered if I would ever be able to master telepathic speech, since my brain was less dense and therefore less complex. Then Sally suddenly appeared before me, dressed in a tight black bodysuit with a bright red hourglass, its neck between her firm, protruding breasts.

She wore shiny black pointed toe stiletto-heel knee-high boots. The mask on her face covering her eyes had eight legs that extended and latched behind her head. Her dreadlocks were covered by a black wig, pulled back in a long ponytail. *I had never seen a woman so sexy!*

"I knew you'd be wearing black," she said. "At least we match."

We didn't match. She was the huge singularity, while I was the tiny male, trembling at the edge of Sally's web.

"I checked all over the Internet," I said. "I couldn't find a Mothfest event for today in LA. Is this a private party?"

"No, it's very public. In fact, they're expecting over 100,000 humans this year—the biggest crowd ever. Are you ready?"

"Sure," I answered, nervous all at once.

"I'm going to set your control panel so that I can control your phasing from my mini-console. All I need you to do is follow me—walk behind me until I get us to a point where we can safely teleport. You can do that?"

"Yes," I nodded, nauseous.

*****

I began to see an enormous, circular, glass-paneled building before me as Sally held my hand, leading me. And yet, I was still in the living room of my apartment. Looking up, I read the words: *Los Angeles Convention Center*. Huge crowds were amassed all around the building, awaiting admittance, but Sally and I walked through them—we literally walked through people until we got to the glass door entrance, and then we walked through the glass.

We traveled through a corridor as all around us, humans in costume bustled along, some stopping to strike poses for pictures and others disappearing into conference rooms. One colorful, panting couple was having sex in a remote bathroom stall.

I remember seeing a Spiderman-chick, a Jean-Luc Picard, a Wonder Woman, a Chewbacca, a vampire queen and a realistic Borg drone as Sally led me through a one-foot-thick wall into a private room. I was confused, because I still was in my living room. I saw and felt both places, blurring back and forth.

"We'll have thirty seconds to find our target location," she said. "Commence teleport."

*****

The was no puff of smoke, no bang, no aurora borealis/ionization effect. My living room just abruptly disappeared, and I was in a dim and empty room, alone with Sally, feeling woozy, queasy, struggling to stand. My head was hurting—I could feel the pulsing vessels in my brain, could feel the strain, the throbbing as I fell.

I woke with a start, my head in Sally's lap.

"How long was I asleep?"

"Almost an hour—not bad for your first teleport. You'll be wobbly on your legs for about fifteen minutes, so let me know when you're ready to go out and have some fun. Let's get this party started!"

"Where are we?"

"You couldn't tell when we came in? We're at Comic-Con—Nerds, at least ten thousand, begging to be eaten. Cosplay at its best! It's *Mothfest* for draugar!"

Sally had a pair of glasses that allowed her to see through the walls when she had them on, so after I recuperated and was ready to join Mothfest, she found a deserted hallway where we could enter undetected. Within seconds after we were in the crowded hallways and auditoriums, the moths began to appear—some even dressed as moths.

Tony Stark/Iron Man (suit, glasses, hair and porn moustache) stopped in his tracks upon seeing Sally, but she grabbed my hand and walked on, ignoring him. A phoney-looking, rotting male draugr tried to follow us, but she shoved him hard, sending him tumbling toward a wall.

It seemed "Mothfest" at Comic-Con was already a well-established sub-culture. There were several women, obviously trying to portray themselves as draugar, strolling down the corridors, though none compared with the actual draugar there, who seemed to radiate an unmistakable presence and attracted fawning male admirers. Bane from Batman and The Hamburglar were following Sally, and then a Klingon and Drax the Destroyer came along. *Ridiculous!* Deadpool and Catwoman were obviously a couple.

The fog cleared from my head and my legs became steady as I tried to keep up. It seemed Sally had a specific area she wanted to occupy, and she was in a hurry to get there. When Kylo Ren tried to block her path to get her attention, we phased right through him and then a wall.

I realized why Sally was in such a rush to get to the pillar at the center of the convention when I saw who was already there. A human Daenerys Targaryen knelt before the draugar royal, bowing.

Astrid held court as the red punk queen, wearing a red wig and red corset with intricate black-lace on the front panels and a frilly red-lace mini-skirt with red stiletto boots. The bodice narrowed her waist to surreal proportions while the bustier presented perfectly-round, firm, full, exaggerated breasts to a crowd of devotees who hooted and reacted to her every pose, all eyes following a red glowing spider tattoo on her chest.

She held a stiff, three-foot-long braided black leather rod in her hand, which she used to direct her groveling, sycophantic followers. Her silk mask was red and framed in black lace spider-legs, like Sally's, while she wore dark blue lipstick.

After eight hundred-ninety-two-years, Astrid had attained physical perfection for the draugar body. The musculature beneath her smooth, tan, unblemished skin rivaled human female bodybuilders, though distinctly shapelier and more feminine. Her calves, thighs, pelvis, arms, back and shoulders were perfectly-proportioned, designed to stimulate libido and delight the eyes.

I had to look away to clear my mind, to maintain my sanity. I remember thinking, *I know what she is*, while I pitied the fifty-something fawning followers who, unwitting, flew directly toward her fatal flame.

"*I'd trade them all for you!*" she said into my mind, her lips unmoving as she spoke. "*Forget my sister. Just relax and let me show you how I'm better than she is. I'll come to you again tonight.*"

I looked over at Sally, who did not react to her sister's proposition, so I concluded telepathic speech could be specific, or direct, based on the individual.

"*Don't look at me,*" Astrid abruptly warned, "*as it will let my sister know that you can hear me speak. I have the answers to the questions bothering you. Besides, I'm over thrice her age. What Sally offers, I can offer more.*"

"*You're listening to my sister?*" Sally asked. "*Stand on the other side of me. Don't even look at her!*"

"I've never done this before," I complained aloud. "How can I *not* listen?"

"*I just forbade her not to talk to you unless she also shares her words with me. She just reluctantly agreed. That conniving bitch!*"

"Uni telam, uni aranea,"[22] Astrid then said to both of us. *"If he stays here, he's mine."*

Apparently, Astrid had secured the best draugar location available at the convention center—a wide swath of high traffic space between the Talent and the Main Stage, not far from the Autograph Table. She stood amidst a complement of handsome men of various races and body types. I was certain that one of the men (dark, muscular, 6'4", crew-cut, dressed as Black Panther) played football for USC, where he wore the "69" jersey.

A few minutes later, there were at least seventy men crowded around her, entranced, competing for a word, a glance, a smile. Aranea Highwind, serving as servant to Astrid, was certainly a draugr.

Sally pulled me back to a safe distance, and we watched as a spellbound convention interviewer approached Astrid, eyes struggling to focus on her face rather than her incredible body. Grinning, he held up the microphone, glancing nervously at the burgeoning entourage around her.

"And who are you?" he asked.

"Rhianna, Inanna—Queen Anna to you. The Red Queen."

"Queen?" he asked. "Queen of where, or what?"

"Queen of Draugars, silly human child. Who are you? Will you be my next meal?"

"I will if you want me to be," he laughed. "I'm Trevor Lord, and I'm here at the request of the event host, who wants to get some of the more remarkable characters and costumes on camera for promotional purposes. What character are you dressed as?"

"Myself."

"Yourself? And you're a character from where? I've got nerd cred, and I don't recognize you. Spiderwoman? The Red Widow? Are you comics? Graphic novels? Anime?"

"I'm a creature from your dreams... and your nightmares."

"What are your special powers?"

"Superiority over humans, science and technology. I devour human males, most of them much better than you are. I love

---

[22] Latin – *One web, one spider*

Mothfest, where I can speak my truth, can share my purpose honestly and no one bats an eye. I simply love it here!"

"Mothfest? I hafta say," Trevor said, backing a bit to get a better look at her outfit and body, "you have to be the hottest woman at the convention—or any convention I've been to—and as I can see, you have a loyal following. Any chance our promoters'll be able to sign you to a talent contract?"

"Never, Trevor," she retorted. "I don't need the distraction, but you're welcome to hang out and party with us later on. We're just getting started."

"*Trevor's already dead,*" Sally said to me, though without speaking. "*Astrid's always had a way with human males. Ironic—probably because she hates them more than anyone I've known. I'll find another place to spin my web.*"

*****

As we scouted a location, I saw another female draugar posted at the far end of the exhibit booths. This tan-skinned draugr was dressed as Lewis Carroll's Alice, and while she didn't have quite the draw that Astrid had, there had to be about twenty men and ten women lurking around and following her, eager to *go down her rabbit hole.*

"*That's Karma,*" Sally said. "*She's our youngest sister, 200-years-old. She's progressive and authentic—without the bitterness that sort of creeps in if you haven't found a balance after a hundred years. She has a human female lover who's cool with her coming here and being gone for most of Gormánuður, but I suppose she doesn't have much of a choice.*"

"Other than your father, are all draugar female?" I asked.

"*A little less than one hundred are male. My father, along with seventy of his researchers and their assistants are male, though there are a few males randomly spread out among global human populations. Then there's rumor of one ancient African male draugr who they say is older than my father. They say he's some 3,000 years, but he has possibly transcended to another realm, one bordering divinity.*"

"One hundred males then, compared to over 143,000 females? Either males aren't being born or someone's killing them."

"Draugar males born to draugar mothers were always extremely rare, and even successful term pregnancies faced high neonatal and perinatal mortality rates. There are very few fertile draugar males—it's our draugar vulnerability. Without new blood, there'll be no more draugar born as babies, and with the ongoing divergence of draugar and human DNA, no more draugar will emerge through the blood exchange, or comingling, because no humans will survive."

In minutes, Sally found a suitable convention place to occupy, though there was yet another draugr female, toying with a cloud of male moths perhaps one hundred feet away. The other female, recognizing Sally's rank and danger in proximity, first hissed and yielded to a place where we no longer saw her face or web.

As soon as Sally stopped and took her place, the human males began to congregate around her web display, while swarming in. Most seemed too nervous to approach, though one began by bringing *vin sanglant*, while others showed devotion, offering their throats, submitting to her will. I stood back in the distance, watching in bewilderment.

"However, on extremely rare occasions, there have been random human males and females born to human mothers with various levels of draugar DNA. Your mother did not know it, but half her DNA was draugar. Your father may have been a draugar hybrid, rare indeed. The odds of them coming together were statistically infrequent, nearly impossible.

"I estimate your DNA is between 40 and 45% draugar. You're not draugar, but you're not completely human either. As a result, you have a better chance of surviving the comingling exchange, and if you do, it's possible that you can be the progenitor of a whole new generation of draugar children born to female draugar. Do you understand?"

I was incapable of answering, though I nodded my head as I approached, and pushing through dozens of awestruck men crowded around her, I took her hand and whispered in her ear.

"What are you doing, Sally? What's this all about? Why did you really bring me here?"

"So you could understand that you are more to me than just another meal, so you could recognize that I'm in love with you. You see the human males who crowd around!

"They're in a mortal competition, within bitter rivalry to be consumed by me, and were I vapid, I would watch and choose the biggest, strongest, handsome, most intelligent and most determined male to eat, as many other draugar females do, though some prefer the female human species to the male.

"But I have spent my life in search of something more, and you can help me to attain it if you love me in eternity. I brought you here so you would know the truth in certainty. In spite of all the moths who fly to me, I wish to be with you, and only you."

*****

And it was true—she could have taken any of the eighty men and women circling, fawning, flailing headstrong toward her flame, which she apparently had done for many years. And only then, I realized why she had chosen me. Humans crave eternal life, though having it, she wanted something more.

But she had said something earlier that put me at ill-ease. She said that I was not completely human—that my DNA had partial-draugar genes. While I did not completely understand the implication, I began to realize my sacrifice would factor in the destiny of draugary.

"I'm finished choosing from the best. Tonight, we celebrate the ides of Gormánuður! My sister, will you come? And will you bring your prey?" the voice of Astrid said into my head.

"I will not come to celebrate," Sally replied. *"We came to Mothfest so that he would know that I had other options and I could have easily chosen someone else."*

"Then sister, by all means, he needs to come and to experience the Draugar Ball—especially if you're convinced that he'll survive, especially if he's going to our world to celebrate the Seiðr ritual."

"The Draugar Ball?" I asked.

"You don't wanna go. Believe me."

"If I'm going to Greenland with you for Seiðr, I need to know. I want to go."

*****

We teleported to a place in the valley, which was an isolated medieval European-fashioned chateau on a large estate, maybe some 15,000 square-feet. At the convention center, I barely blinked my eyes and we were standing in the huge ballroom, surrounded by people with headphones who were dancing, though I heard no music.

The headphones glowed in different colors—red, green and blue. Apparently, the color-coded music was beamed directly to individuals—three wild and crazy parties in one room! There had to be at least two thousand humans there, all dancing, twerking, grinding in a seeming primitive, erotic ritual.

There were bartenders making drinks and servers passing *vivant-sang-chaud* in champagne flutes. Sally took a glass and handed me another.

"You wanted to experience the Draugar Ball? Well, here we are. Enjoy the experience. Take up the draugr grail and sip the sacred secret of eternity!"

I watched my vegan girlfriend as she sipped the redolent dark burgundy elixir from the flute and licked her dripping lips. I'd had a few drinks at Mothfest, but I was certain I would not be able to stomach warm, living human blood. Beyond that, I was appalled that servers were offering it. *Where did it come from? Were draugar slaughtering humans in another room?* So now I knew that Sally, like Astrid, was drinking human blood!

"What's with all the women here?" I asked. "I thought all the draugar at Mothfest were female, and they only eat men."

"The many human females selected at Mothfest are for the seventy priestly princes who never leave the science and research facility back home, and for their assistants. My father choses his own—always a bitchy, gold-digging ingénue."

As I looked around, many others were partaking of the blood cocktail—even the humans. The party was wild, frenetic, teetering on the narrow edge where reality met the surreal. There was a purple draugar concoction in a shot glass that was a powerful human aphrodisiac. The environment itself was a drug, making me dizzy. Sally gently placed her warm crystal glass against my lips, stroking my face, and cautiously, I took a sip. *Odd, I felt instantly intoxicated!*

There were many rooms in the chateau, and I took note of the procession of draugar females taking males and females upstairs into the rooms and never returning. Judging from the level of sexual excitement in the room, I guessed the draugar were engaging their carefully-selected partners in sex and teleporting their comatose bodies to another location. Sally confirmed my suspicion.

*****

Minutes later, a group of naked men carried a large, sculptured, solid-gold clawfoot bathtub down the spiral staircase—among those, the USC linebacker. After they placed it at the center of the ballroom floor, I could see it was filled with warm blood. By my calculations, sixteen men had been sacrificed in order to fill that tub.

Astrid stood at the center of the torch and candle-lit room, nodding in approval as the men stepped aside. She was dressed as Isis: lotus staff in her right hand, ankh in her left, wings of eagle feathers draped from her arms. She wore a menat necklace, fashioned from precious stones, and a headdress depicting the horns of a cow with a solar disc between them. Upon Astrid's appearance, all the headphones in the room came off.

"All hail the bathing of the daughter of the Siren goddess Sekhmet, celebrated on our Seiðr's Eve!"

So that is when I realized Astrid was naturally an African. We watched a copper-skinned Queen Anna then remove her headdress, necklace and her clothing. Naked and without shame, she walked to the tub and slipped into the warm crimson liquid to her neckline. After a minute, she languorously extended her foot and leg, pointing her toes, and then the other.

The bloodbath lasted perhaps five minutes as she performed a series of ritualistic movements with her hands, legs and head. Then she stood, blood coating, oozing, trailing, dripping from her shoulders and arms, her breasts, hips and thighs, and she struck a familiar Isis pose as an attendant replaced the headdress, menat necklace and wings.

*****

Suddenly Sally and I were in the living room of my apartment and I had a sick stomach, along with a headache. Captivated by Astrid's exhibition, I was not prepared for the transport and vomited on my living room carpet, startled as I noted it contained some of the blood I had consumed minutes earlier.

"What happened?" I asked. "Why are we back here?"

"I couldn't take any more of my sister," Sally spoke aloud. "Besides, I could see you lusting her. She would have come after you."

"And I would have rejected her," I said. "I can make my own choices!"

"You're weak and male. You are incapable of choice. You could not have resisted her."

"I *have* resisted her—I resisted her yesterday morning. Stop deciding for me! You think you know me, but you *don't*."

"I'm sorry," she sighed. "It's just that Astrid always does this to me. I came so close with Rai!"

"I'm not Rai. What exactly happened with him?"

"I know he loved me," Sally said, "and yet Astrid exerts a strange, enticing power over human males. Perhaps it is because she hates them ardently, or she can read their minds— but none have yet resisted her. That's why I tried to hide you all along, to keep you from her power and her charms. If we're not vigilant, she will seduce you and devour you before our promising though unassured comingling.

"It was the same with Rai. We were together for one month, until we went to Mothfest, up until the Draugar Ball—and on that night, he went to her. He *chose* her over me. Admittedly, he wasn't as compatible, but he was close. She cruelly, painfully devoured him, *without* comingling, and left his body at my condo door. Then next she called the FBI, accusing me of murdering Rai, of murdering many other men."

"Why does she do this wickedness to you?" I asked. "Astrid's your older sister. Why does she hate you so much?"

"I will not lie to you. Two hundred years ago, when I was young and foolish, once there was a certain human male whom Anna loved. Back then, she was a draugr, sweet and hopeful, and she was the apple of our father's eye. She told this human everything. She shared her heart and hope and vulnerability. She wasn't jaded then—so different than the hater she became!"

Contrite, remembering, how Sally wept! "Astrid was so delighted that her human male survived comingling, though she was twice the age that I am now. However, when the man she loved began to lust for me, to secretly proclaim eternal love for me, I balked, and yet I yielded to his flattery. I never had received solicitation from a draugar male, so I was curious..."

"Don't tell me you slept with the love of your sister's life?" I groaned, but Sally would not answer. Instead, she vanished from my living room, obviously ashamed.

"*It was so wrong, a horrible betrayal,*" Sally wept, while speaking in my head, "*It happened just one time. So feeling guilty and repentant, realizing his mistake, he weeping did confess his sin to furious Astrid, who killed and then devoured him immediately. And since that time, she does not hide her animosity for males, and yet she hates me more. We put on niceties since we are family, although I know that she would kill me if she could.*

"*One web, one spider. I violated sacred Draugar Law. I was so sorry! I've tried to make it up to her two hundred years, but she's incapable of clemency. A foolish curiosity fulfilled to stain my history! An empty exercise! A story written long ago. My reputation ruined by a lusting, newly-founded draugar male!*"

October 28 – Closing Arguments

With Sally gone, I tried to still my thoughts, I tried to understand the things I'd seen and heard that night. I thought I should prepare myself for Greenland and Seiðr, which certainly included draugar ceremonies of comingling. She wanted to stay to protect me from Astrid, but I demanded solitude. *I could feel it*—I was stronger, smarter. I felt more energized. It must have been the blood I drank while at the Draugar Ball.

If I was partially a draugr, then naturally my first experience with drinking living human blood would have a powerful effect on me. My body tingled, even at the level of my cells. I felt a craving that I'd never known. *To think that now I lusted humam blood!*

"*Come out to me!*" a female voice repeated in my head. It was Astrid. "*I'm on the street outside your home. Please come and talk to me, please come outside. We've never been alone before tonight.*"

I swirled the half-filled champagne flute within my hand, and feeling bold, I swallowed what was left and licked the glass.

"If I come out, you'll want to eat me," I called back, "like you devoured Rai last year!"

"*A wicked and pernicious lie! Do not be fooled, my little boy. I never ate him, and I won't eat you. He begged to be my mate, but your conniving, jealous Sally ate him anyway. My sister does not always tell the truth.*

"*She takes advantage of your lust and gullibility. She knows that you cannot distinguish good and bad and makes you think she is benevolent. In truth, she slanders me in treachery, because she knows that I, Astrid, am good—she lies to hide and to disguise her latent wickedness.*"

"Your golden statue," I demanded. "There beside my Jeep I filled a metal vat with water, since I knew that you would come tonight. I need to see you put your statue in the vat, because I know the statue is your link to Draugar-built technologies, and water severs those abilities. So if you really want to talk to me, I think I need to watch you put the statue in."

"You didn't come to know the Draugar mysteries by accident or on the onion Internet, so if my sister told you secret sacraments, she's violated Draugar law and will be punished for her crimes."

"Your sister Sally didn't tell me that," I said, "but if you want to talk to me, you'll put the statue in. However, you must place it first against your heart—the eyes must glow for authenticity."

"Who told you that?" she asked, *"since those are mysteries that only Draugar understand, and lowly humans shouldn't know such things!"*

"It doesn't matter how I know. I need to see the glowing eyes and when the statue is submerged, I'll then come out to talk to you. We'll have a level playing field."

"Just shut your snout and come outside! Your queen is here. You dare to make her wait!"

I watched her as she pulled the statue close, which caused its eyes to glow, and then she eased it down into the tub. And so I exited my home, but only after she had moved some distance from the vat. Then she approached and kissed me on the lips one time, but I would not allow a second kiss.

"You called me out to *talk* to me?"

"I came to save you from my sister's wicked reckoning," she said. "She swears to love you, but she lies. She only wants the spark from you, the opportunity to be divine so she can punish me and all the enemies she's made through lies and treachery."

She held two slender glasses in her hands, two champagne flutes, half-filled with still-warm human blood, and handing one to me, she offered a *verre relevé.*[23]

"To Seiðr and to what will come tomorrow night!"

"What's that?" I asked while sipping from my glass. "You have not gone to Seiðr for two hundred years."

"I'll go to right what's wrong, reclaim my proper place and what is mine, to make a case for who should rule the Earth."

My glass half-gone, I felt a tingling in my arms and legs, a surging in my chest, a burning in my brain. Initially, I thought

---

[23] French – *raised glass*

that I'd been drugged, but no—it was the blood and its effect on me, which made me ravenous and bold.

"What do you want, Astrid?" I asked.

"So many years ago, my sister took from me the greatest object of my love—my human-turned-to-draugr mate, so all I seek is recompense. She has apologized, but guilty, unfelt words will not suffice. She must replace my loss, and only then will I forgive."

"I'm human, but I'm not some object anyone could barter with or give as recompense. I said. "My destiny is my own choice."

"You fool," she sighed. "The choice was made for you when you decided not to run. You're under Draugar jurisdiction now—your fate to be decided by our laws. I haven't celebrated Seiðr for two hundred years, but on tomorrow, I'll go back to make my legal case. Our destinies are now entwined."

"But I love Sally," I protested. "I could not love you even if I wanted to."

"It isn't wise to love a singularity that you don't have capacity to understand. You cannot see her web? I trust that you will come to love me over time—when you have gained more insight and experience, when you're no longer hindered or encumbered by mortality." She took my face within her hands. "You fight it, but you're lusting me. I see it in your eyes and feel it in your kiss. It grows within your loins. Succumb to me!"

She held me tight and kissed my lips again, this time with well-positioned fingers pressed along my spine—the way that Sally did within my carnal dreams in bed. Whatever she was doing caused immediate arousal in my groin and fluctuation in my heart.

I felt myself succumbing, weakening, but I remembered Rai, and summoning my will, I broke from her embrace. The blood I drank had given me the strength to separate from her. I grabbed her wrists and shoved to send her flying to the ground some twenty feet away.

Before I could react, she once again was close, restraining me, was struggling to master me, but for a second time, I felt a surge of strength and held her helpless in submission with my steady arms.

"What has my sister done to you!" she screamed while there she thrashed and strained, both angered and surprised. "An ordinary human cannot be so strong!"

"Yet here we are!" I mocked, and looking in her eyes, I saw a creature vulnerable and frightened for a first and only time in centuries, which deep within my heart excited me. The irresistible Astrid—so beautiful and dangerous... with now the tables turned. I pulled her close and forced a kiss upon her luscious lips, which still retained the scent and taste of human blood.

She fought initially, until I forced a second kiss, and then a third. And then her fingers found their sensual positions on my vertebrae, while I found mine along her back. Astrid submitted as our lower bodies tangled, pressed together, found a rhythmic synchronicity, back and forth, an ebb and flow, and as she moaned aloud in ecstasy, I clutched her shoulders, pushing her away.

"Our fates are sealed," she said. "You only met my sister so that you would be enmeshed with me! Your kisses burn within my brain! I *tasted* our compatibility! Come home with me! Comingle with me now!"

"By nature, I am drawn to you," I said, while turning her away, "but nature is not master over me. I've chosen Sally, and I've proven to myself tonight that I will soon become a singularity to engineer my separate destiny. The draugar have no power over me, no jurisdiction in my fate."

"So foolish and so arrogant!" she laughed. "How dare you think to run away from my advance! No male has ever overcome my web! You can't escape. You'll never be a singularity—you're just a common and occasional irregularity within a race of ants! Tomorrow you shall see how small and insignificant you are as humans on the Earth!"

*****

"She came to me and I resisted her," I said to Sally on the phone. "I'm not afraid of her."

"Your haughtiness is ill-advised tonight," she answered me. "She's been a force of nature since the the birth of Timbuktu. Astrid's a cunning spider set against a single ant without defense. I mean, seriously—you didn't realize that she would know what you were going to say for fifteen seconds in advance, before you even thought to say a word?

"And she can read your mind! She could have torn you, limb from limb. I am her equal in the flesh, and yet I tremble in her presence, rightfully in fear of her. You risked your life for puerile arrogance. We're fortunate that you are still alive!"

"Astrid—" I said, "she told me you've been lying to me all this time, that you were using me, like you were using Rai. She said that all the love that you've professed for me is nothing but an act—the web you use to trap your males, as you have done for many years. And then she said you've slandered her, portrayed her as an evil and rebellious draugar daughter, feared and hated in your realm.

"'Appearances deceive,' she said, insisting she was light, while you are darkness, opposite of what you trained me to believe.' And finally, she told me that you stole the object of her love, that you betrayed your sister for your carnal-lust. You stole her echo and her only chance for happiness."

Then Sally re-appeared at once within my living room. She tried to kiss me, but I pulled away.

"I told you what I did," she said, "which I confess has cast a shadow on my reputation— though however, what I did was not for carnal-lust. I was a victim of my innocence and youthful curiosity. I sinned against my sister, so I'm in her debt, although I realize to my regret: *not even God can change the past.* What's done is done, and one mistake will not define my life. *I wonder why she let you live?"*

"She had no choice."

"Don't be a fool—*of course she did!* She could have eaten you in spite of what advantage you perceived you had. She only let you live because she has devised a plan."

"She's going to Seiðr tomorrow..." I announced from sudden memory, "'to make her case before her father and the Draugar world,' she said."

Sally seemed shocked and confused, but she was angry at me for disregarding her warning and having engaged her sister.

"I should have warned that your initial taste of blood would make you drunk, would falsely make you feel empowered and invulnerable. You are excused for that because you were intoxicated, *but tomorrow to Seiðr? To make her case to whom?* Did she provide a reason why?"

A little less intoxicated, I was loath to tell her that Astrid had said she wanted me as recompense. *What tangled webs we weave!* Instead I told a lie and said I didn't know.

"She could have eaten you tonight, yet she refrained," she said, "and more profound—she has not gone to Seiðr for two hundred years! And only now she goes?"

"She says she goes 'because you slandered her and fouled her name and life, because you stole her favor in your father's eyes, in Draugar eyes, and finally, because you robbed her of a single opportunity for love in perpetuity.'"

"And you *believe* the things she said?" a sad, deflated Sally asked through swelling tears.

"What do I know?" I asked. "I'm nothing but a lowly human male, an ignorant ant who cannot see the spiderweb. For spiders, ants exist to be consumed. Why does it matter what I think?"

She grabbed my shoulders as she sought my eyes.

"Because I love you more than anyone I've loved before, and more than anyone I'll ever love again."

"And do you say that to them all?" I asked, "the ants—the human males you eat? Is that the spell you cast? Is *love* the web you weave? You never gave me choice. That first day in the coffee shop—you trapped me on that day! You studied me. You took advantage of my gullibility!"

I heard myself in my own voice, and yet the words and sentiment were from spoken in my still-intoxicated state. *I still was drunk from drinking living human blood!*

"You're serious?" she asked. "Ten minutes with my sister and you've changed your mind about the life we planned? And all the time we spent together—twenty-seven days—means nothing to you now? The many nights we spent in amorous embrace? What did my sister say to disincline your heart toward me? What wicked spell has overwhelmed your thoughts?

"I'm wounded, hurt, astounded and betrayed forevermore. I offered you my soul and all the love and loyalty that I possessed within my heart—a willing draugar sacrifice— unvalued, devastated and denied."

Astrid was right—my destiny did not belong to me. I stood there drunk, unable to respond. I wanted to recant the hurtful words that issued from my mouth against my will. I wanted to profess my love and loyalty for Sally, but my thinking was suppressed, and only then I realized blood-drunkenness and arrogance (and possibly Astrid) were in possession of my tongue.

"A sweet and sticky web, and such a whore to steal your sister's mate!" I said. "And when I'm gone, I'm sure you'll quickly find another foolish human male to eat."

I watched as Sally wept her final tears, and then I saw the change, beginning in her angry eyes.

"How dare you say those things to me! I loved you more than you could understand, and more than you deserved. I loved you more than life itself, but now that love has been undone. How dare you undervalue all I offered you!" she sobbed again. "But now I know with certainty you are unworthy of my love, so it has been withdrawn. Tomorrow, I will go alone to Seiðr, but I will not eat, so in the sequel, you've betrayed yourself and love, and you have lost a worthy prize!"

Then she was gone, and when I looked outside beside my door, her statue was not there. Alone, I felt a sense of *déjà vu*. It seemed I was repeating a scenario that happened to the day, one year before.

For all that mattered, I was living (or reliving) poor Rai's final hours, and the outcome, whether same or disparate, would be determined—not by differences in what we chose, but what we willed.

I hoped that she could hear my thoughts and tried to speak to her through auditory nerve implant, but still I had not mastered speech. For twenty-seven days we grew together— now we were apart, and all because I didn't listen when she warned me to avoid Astrid.

By then, it did not matter who was telling me the truth, and who was good or bad, since only love was relevant. I willed that Sally over time would realize the words I spoke were not my own, that we would go to Seiðr and comingle as we planned.

*****

When Mel appeared, I worried she was actually Astrid, appearing in this guise, and unprotected, she would have her way with me. A kiss confirmed identity. Melpomene had come to me. My Muse had once again returned.

"By now you've realized that, as a mortal human, you cannot distinguish good and bad," she said, *"but I was born divine. Because you didn't listen and you strayed, you've stabbed yourself with many pains. I tried to save you for myself and from your destiny. Mais maintenant, les jeux sont faits—the die is cast, the games are done."*

"I'm sorry, Mel," I ruefully confessed, "I couldn't help myself. I thought that I could choose, but choice is false as you have said, and mortal life is merely exercise. When Sally gave me opportunity, I should have run."

"It would have made no difference, since divinity has planned your fate. Your 'running' represented choice, which was irrelevant. No matter what you did, the end would be the same, and you would be exactly where you are tonight. Despite your efforts and my intervention, you could not escape this predicated destiny."

"If choice does not exist?" I asked, "then what's the purpose of humanity? If I am meant 'to be like God,' a god-like progeny, then I alone should choose my destiny."

"No, you were never meant 'to be like God,' but rather to reflect omniscient qualities. So you, a fleshly mortal, must submit and seek to merge your choice in order to pursue a higher

will. Humanity can only choose to carry out omniscient purposes, so what you choose must in the end comport with order in the universe."

"Then why do I have intellectual ability?" I asked. "I'd rather be a salmon or an ant, a thoughtless drone, completely engineered to carry out my role within the greater scheme, *without* ability to choose."

"Your intellectual ability exists to help you carry out omniscient purposes, and yours as well, if they have been aligned. Consider Jonah, son of Amittai: his foolish choices were irrelevant. Against his will, he thoroughly achieved a greater will, a lesson meant to help you understand why you are here tonight, so agitated and confused."

"And angry too!" I shouted then. "What am I here to do?"

"Fulfill your destiny, but there are those opposing destiny divine, who seek to thwart what you are meant to do, and they become your enemies. There is no good or bad in this, but only those who, willing or unwilling, seek a higher purpose, and there are those who don't."

"But I can only think of Sally now. I didn't mean to say those awful words to her, but now she's gone. I love her and to be with her is all I want, but if I cannot have her, I just want to die, and I will not cooperate with destiny."

"I absolutely am convinced that Sally loves you too," Mel said, *"though fate has chosen separate destinies for you. Therefore, your love, however full of passion or profound, perhaps is not enough. For both of you, your sheer determination must exceed your love."*

"And what of you and me, my Muse and spirit mate?" I asked. "Is wanting Sally a betrayal of the love we've shared? And is my desperate plea for intervention from divinity unfair? I'll always love you, Mel, and still I beg your help to prove my love."

"Omniscience and the bounds of destiny inform that I should give you up for now, but I will always be within your whispered voice until your final breath.

"In two days' time, you'll face a final test that will determine if you live or die. I'll help you if I can, but you must not forget— you must remember that I am the Muse of Tragedy."

October 29 – The New Garden and the Tower

A portent early in the day: my skin began to glow a slightly bioluminescent bluish-green, like foxfire in the woods. An hour after that, someone remotely activated on my wrist the panel Sally had implanted there.

I spent the morning calling her to no avail, and then I drove to check her condo, knocking on the door, but she was not at home. I couldn't feel her presence there. Just one day earlier, we'd planned on going to Seiðr together for initiation and comingling, and yet today she went alone, or with another human male.

I was at fault. I foolishly ignored her warning, listened to Astrid and drank with her, so I was dealing with the consequence. Somehow, I lost possession of my tongue and said the spiteful words that stung remorseful Sally's soul, and words that played upon her guilt. At last, Astrid succeeded in her purpose. She exacted her revenge, took recompense by using me to break her sister Sally's heart.

Mel told me I would face a test in two days' time, and what she said—-along with activation of the panel at my wrist— informed that somehow, I would go Seiðr for the ceremony. With Sally gone, I thought for sure Astrid would visit me to do malevolence, but no, I couldn't feel her presence either on that day. I closed my eyes, and feeling neither her nor Mel, I then awaited destiny. I contemplated the effect of immortality on trials yet to come.

One moment I was in my living room, while in another, I was in a huge cavernous space, its ceiling more than ninety meters high, and back and forth I went until I saw myself an ant or something less, reduced to humbling irrelevance. I struggled, trying not to vomit up my breakfast, realizing I was being teleported to another place.

*****

My skin glowed bluish-green, while I could feel the straining throbbing veins within my brain, and as my eyes began to focus, I realized that I was in a seeming garden, and there were trees and vegetation all about the place, a futuristic tower in the background, and there was a host who greeted me.

"I knew you'd come," he said, "I'm certain you remember me. By now, you must have many questions and concerns."

I recognized his face. The man who greeted me was Erick Draugar, smiling as he shook my hand.

"Where am I? first of all," I asked.

"In southern Greenland, sixty meters under Earth and in a hollow, spanning eight kilometers in width and length. The ceiling is one hundred meters high."

"I can't be underground?" I countered then. "I see the sun!"

"You see *a* sun, a perfect replica, exact by draugar ingenuity," he laughed, "but certainly you know by now that engineering's our advantage and our strength. The ice above the the ground is at a minimum two thousand meters thick."

"My skin is glowing bluish-green. What does that mean?"

"It's human DNA that glows beneath our fabricated sun and moon and stars—a cautionary measure necessary over time. Occasionally, we have visitors from above."

It truly was a garden, all lush and green with trees and ripened fruit that ranged from apples, oranges, pomegranates, grapes, persimmons, peaches, melons, mangos and bananas. There were taller trees and vines and cold and crystal flowing streams. I saw delightful butterflies and vibrant-colored birds and heard the sound of frogs, cicadas and the rustling of active animals within the undergrowth.

"How beautiful!" I sighed in overawe. "I've never seen the like!"

"We recreated it," he laughed, "no disrespect to the original. There even is a rare, unusual tree that flourishes and grows somewhere within the garden midst, which symbolizes choice."

I looked again and saw a shiny marble tower in the background—saw it reaching up into the clouds.

"And why so tall a building in a finite space?" I asked.

"Symbolic effort, joining earth and sky, the physical and spiritual, intangible and tangible, divine-inspired and divinity. As yet, it's not complete, but we are working constantly to get it done."

"A modern tower in the modern city, I suspect," I said, "but why? What is the purpose of this place?"

"A tower is symbolically a link or conduit," he answered me, "our reaching out and striving for divinity."

Then Erick nodded, patted on my shoulder as he directed me along.

"You cannot understand it all, my son," he laughed. "not in one day what's taken nineteen hundred years to build. Just predispose your mind to take it in. You didn't come with Sally, so I volunteered to be your guide."

*****

There was a grassy knoll within an open area before the tower in the distance, and in that space, I saw the giant statue of a spider on a pedestal. Its back six legs were resting on the earth, the other two held up in salutation, touching the antennae of a giant ant.

"You're really stuck on that analogy," I laughed, "the spider and the ant."

"But not just any spider. *Zodariellum surprisum.*"

"'Surprise em?' Right... no way," I said. "You can't be serious."

"This spider species lives within the colony, although the ants cannot distinguish there are spiders in their midst. They prey upon the ants, though they would not consume the queen and do not take enough to make a difference."

We headed toward the tower looming closer. As we walked along, I saw that there were others glowing bluish-green, the human guests of other draugar reconvened in sacred pilgrimage to celebrate Seiðr.

"I thought I'd come with Sally, but I haven't heard from her. Have you?"

"Of course I have," he said while tapping on his temple, nudging me along. "I know about the problems that you're having, and I'm not surprised—two sisters fighting over you. You'll have to understand the choice you made."

"What choice?" I asked.

"You chose Astrid."

"No! no," I argued. "I rejected her. I love your daughter, Sally. She is why I came."

"I know," he said. "But yet you *chose* Astrid, although you came for Sally, who you love." He nodded, and the doors obeyed. "Come in, and welcome to our home!"

Reluctantly, I stepped into the *rez-de-chaussée*[24] area, which seemed to be a futuristic office lab, while in the distance, in an ample space that occupied the other side of some transparent barrier, there were many seeming men, besmocked in white, who worked at stations and with instruments that seemed like unconventional computers.

Further to the left were scientists conducting various experiments. I saw an orb-like vessel hovering, suspended in mid-air, and saw another disappear and reappear. Along the walls were cubes with doors like elevators, where some scientists were coming in and others going to another place.

The floors were dark and shined like precious stone, and looking all around, I realized there was no dust, no dust at all. *How strange!*

"Black onyx" he explained, as if he read my mind. "It's a protective stone, though rare in such great quantity, and beautiful as well. But welcome, guest, and please enjoy a cognac as a friend, a special *paradis* in amber, called Pénélope—it's average age—two hundred years."

"Sure," I answered as I watched an amber/cognac sculpture and two snifters suddenly appear between us. "Are we really sixty meters under solid rock?" I asked, "its surface under ice and snow, two thousand meters thick?"

"Yes, for our security and for the future of the Earth," he answered. "We've learned from recent history it's best to keep a

---

24 French – *ground floor*

distance from humanity, who we have learned to fear. They murdered draugar in the past. We want no part of them. To humans, we are inaccessible, within the Earth."

*****

"And what are you, their President, or King?"

"By virtue of my age, I am the leader of our race—the eldest—sixteen hundred years. I was born a slave in Carthage and I was a young man when the Vandals finally sacked Rome. A mercenary soldier then, I returned to Scandinavia among the Visigoths, and there eventually I learned the art of building ships.

"That was a time when draugar lived with humans, sometimes breeding, neither knowing they were different races—we were longer-lived. The *nosferatu* also lived within that period, although they were a filthy plague, a scourge upon the Earth.

"Just how we came to realize the miracle of living human blood I don't remember now. Some of the women craved and ate both blood and dirt, and then they strangely did not seem to age. It took a little time, but draugar slowly learned there was a correlation, and in human blood, we found the fountain of eternal youth.

"When neither did we age nor die, the humans turned on us and named us enemies. Outnumbered, many draugar died by human hands and torture rituals, and those who found escape were forced to hide in caves and graveyards, where most humans were afraid to go.

"So over time, we grew aggrieved to understand immortal life required drinking or consuming living human blood. Back then, we didn't realize there was a factor in the blood we could metabolize to have eternal youth and health, although we knew that human sacrifice would be involved. Against our inclination and our principles, we learned to be a violent race in order to supply our need for human blood, and after we responsibly had harvested the local human populations, then we set our eyes for fresher prey and learned the value of sustainability, and we embraced diversity.

"Always the story was the same: the humans came to understand that we were different and predatory, so they murdered us, they burned us at the stake, decapitated us. We had to flee in order to survive, and so we then established draugar settlements within the Arctic Archipelago. And yet, the humans hunted us, and they became our existential threat, so our survival was an act of God.

"An intervention on the Earth, divine in nature, was required to preserve our fate—a fiery comet fifteen hundred years ago that caused all human crops to fail and summer frost that brought on plague and pestilence and death, an omen on a flaxen-colored horse, succeeded by a darker beast. The Earth was bathed in twilight for eight hundred years, and in that time, the human race was in decline with plague and famine, hungrily consuming more than we could ever eat."

*****

"In Scandinavia, the humans had already learned the art of building ships, though draugar saw a special value realized by reaching other shores, and so we set our minds to engineering and technology. We built the better ships, maintained the better maps, and since we didn't die, we easily surpassed our human counterparts with our enhanced and our sustained experience. We took our prey from every continent and found and recombined the scattered draugar living all across the Earth.

"On Viking ships that we designed and engineered, we traveled far and wide to capture prey and find our brethren. We sought out knowledge and we made a library of hidden books that sages salvaged from the fires burned in Alexandria and Rome. We dug to find the secrets from the ancient sands of Mesopotamia and the Indus Valley, Tiwanaku and Jericho, Aleppo, Sidon, Anyang and Timbuktu... but more than knowledge, we were seeking out omniscience as a pathway to divinity.

"The *nosferatu* prospered in that age, a pagan, infidel and ignorant race, unlike the noble creatures that you humans have romanticized in novels and your films. Unthinking, like a godless locust swarm, they killed and ate the vulnerable, like savages, and lacking forethought, they consumed the local human populations to exhaustion, spreading sickness and one plague upon another in their wake. Unsanitary in their ways, like rats, they brought on pestilence, contamination and disease. When there was nothing more to eat, the *nosferatu* starved to death, and finally, the remnant that survived until the sun returned could not acclimatize environmental change.

"Yet while the rest on earth existed under darkened skies, our race was working to ignite the light of science and technology and share it with the universe—but every time we sought alliances with humankind, eventually we were betrayed. The humans sought to steal and to extort from us technology that we proposed to freely share, demanding we provide our vulnerabilities and the secrets for destroying us. Humanity is inhumane, the most destructive creature on the planet. They will not relent until 'the draugar threat' has been destroyed.

"For many years, we lived above the surface of the ground, within the Arctic Archipelago. We used a corporate front to hide our purpose and identity. At Draugar Inc., we were the best at building ocean liners and the ships that humans use to cruise between the continents. We specialized at building other vessels too, and utilizing our technology, we flew into the sky and space two hundred years before the early human scientists and engineers considered flight."

"The UFOs we see from time to time!" I sighed. "We thought that they were aliens from other worlds!"

"Not aliens," he said. "You saw the failings in our power grid, the glitches we could not avoid when sharing Earth's magnetic energy. We wanted never to be seen, and we have gotten better over time, although our quantum science will eventually make flying obsolete."

"Your missions when you *have* been seen?" I asked. "What were you doing in our skies?"

"Collecting healthy non-essentials, mapping out the inner Earth," he said. "Most draugar live within the human population and can easily select one human every year for blood exchange. Our seventy researchers here, the princes who have worked for over seven centuries in our labs—the healthy non-essential humans are collected annually in order to provide their living blood exchange."

"And mapping out the inner Earth?" I asked.

"The hollowed spaces here. As long as we were *on* the surface of the Earth," he answered, "we were vulnerable to humans seeking to annihilate our race to steal state-of-the-art technologies. We had to find a sanctuary deep *within* the Earth— away from humankind—a hollow adequate to build a world within a world. So after many decades searching, finally we found this place beneath impenetrable stone and ice. We subsequently took apart our research labs and engineering fabrication sites, and using quantum science, teleported piece by piece into this place.

*****

"This place, of course, required massive energy output, so first our scientists installed our antimatter generators, the genius of the draugar innovative scientific work with antiparticles, and then they fired up reactors that converted antimatter into energy that fueled this draugar paradise and our technologies.

"At first our world was formless, so there was only darkness. Our engineers then fabricated an expanse above, and then a fabricated sun and moon and stars in that expanse, providing day and night. Then next they brought in vegetation of all sorts—the trees and vines and grasses, though they also had to engineer environmental factors, thus creating both a water cycle and a method for infusing oxygen. And then they brought in worms and insects—all the crawling things—before they brought the fish and frogs, the reptiles and the birds. Since space was limited, they did not bring the mammals here, except for female cats."

"How long have you been living in the Earth?" I asked.

"Three human decades at the most, although we measure time in different fundamentals. Time is functionally irrelevant to us, like money for your wealthy humans—Mansa Musa long ago, then Bezos, Buffet and Bill Gates today."

"I'm curious," I said. "Are human governments aware that you exist down here? Do you communicate with any heads of state? Is there a treaty or a pact defining draugar dealings with the human nations of the Earth?"

"In centuries past we did," he answered me, "but we no longer deal with heads of state, because it's obvious that humans cannot choose what's best for them. Instead, we work with secret governmental agencies, and in exchange for science and innocuous technologies, we advocate for peace on Earth, and for environment and maintenance of biological diversity, which benefits us all."

"Then why not live above the ground," I asked, "to make a better Earth?"

"To live among a race of blind and ignorant, ever-agitated, biting, stinging ants?" he laughed. "To arbitrate their senseless arguments. The humans cannot reach us here, so they cannot distract us from our destiny, so we can focus on divinity."

"You want to grant divinity to every draugar on the Earth?" I asked. "To good and wicked draugar, all the same?"

"Divinity cannot be granted," Erick answered me, "since it must be attained, and that is why deserving draugar seek omniscience, which requires oneness with a greater consciousness. So never will the wicked understand or gain divinity."

*****

"And after you have learned to reproduce the hidden factor found in living human blood," I asked, "the spark of immortality—then what will be the destiny of draugarkind?"

"The end is coming soon, though no one knows the day or hour, but in that moment when we generate the spark—when our genetic engineers confirm that draugar immortality is permanent, when draugar have the means to live forever, never needing living human blood—that time will be the *reckoning*. The reckoning will come!"

"The reckoning of what?" I asked.

"Each draugr will be forced to choose," he said, "to either risk their destiny beside the venal, vapid and vexatious ant-like human race, or to withdraw within the Earth, right to this very place, to focus on divinity. And it's a crucial choice, concerning everlasting life, since after every draugr choses. Then we'll close the gate, and those who choose an earthly life cannot return, and we will have no part with them."

"You'll cut them off?" I asked.

"They'll benefit from everlasting immortality, though they will lose the benefit of Draugar science and technology."

"No teleporting? No phasing or manipulating time? No auditory-nerve-implant telepathy?"

"Each being makes a choice:" he answered me, "the *tree of knowledge* or the *tree of life*. In dualistic argument, indeed the female in the garden chose *both* trees, each in a separate reality, and humans are the seed that represent a foolish, egotistic choice, to covet what belongs to God, while draugar issue from the choice to take the fruit of life, in unity with God.

"While envious humans gained by selfishly usurping godly knowledge, they were *mortal* beings, cursed to death, restricting further choice, and so they never found the tree of life. The draugar, on the other hand, when after taking first the godly gift of life, lived long enough to also find the other tree to eat and realize the benefits of knowledge and of life, so draugar choice has been preserved."

"And those who choose to live with humans on the Earth?" I asked. "They represent a conscious choice to take a course and make decisions independently of God?"

"They do not seek omniscience or divinity—are covetous of God—have more in common with their foolish human counterparts. Eventually, omniscient draugar will transcend the bonds of tangibility, and we will seem to disappear, yet we will still exist (though in an altered state), but we will be divine. For those who chose to live with humans on the Earth, they'll share the consequences of humanity on their appointed Judgement Day."

*****

"Why am I here?" I asked to better understand my purpose deep within the Earth.

"My daughter—Sally, as you know her—sought you out, as she believes you are the *Radical,* believes that you possess the spark that is the key to our divinity."

"But I'm a human," I protested, "I know nothing of this spark. How does it work?"

"It goes beyond the science that I understand," he said, "and rests within the realm of the divine. My daughter's theory is that, through comingling—whether you survive or not—that you will share with her the spark that will allow omniscient draugar to attain divinity."

"Do you believe she's right?" I asked.

"Irrelevant. I have another daughter whom you've met," he said, "who challenges her sister's right to you, which is a matter of our draugar jurisprudence. On one hand, I have theory, while on the other, I have law. I love my daughter's equally, which makes this matter problematic to decide. 'The law's an ass,' your Muse, Melpomene, declared."

"And does it matter what I want, or who I want?" I asked.

"It doesn't matter now," he said, "Already, you have made your choice by coming here, a place where you are subject to our laws. You have no legal standing here. In coming, you surrendered choice."

"But you cannot command that I comingle with Astrid, since that would harm my fortune with your other daughter, Sally, who I love—and especially if I survive comingling and I become a draugr and constituent to your law."

"There is no guarantee that you'll survive," he answered, "and as such you're merely prey, or property. I know it seems unfair, but in this jurisdiction, it becomes a purely legal argument. It doesn't matter in the end, since all are subject to the rule of Draugar Law, which binds both you and me. The rest is destiny."

"What are my chances," I inquired, "when comingling with Sally?"

"It is my estimation that with Sally you are ninety-one percent assured you will survive."

"What are my chances with Astrid?"

"No more than fifty-one percent."

"The law aside," I said, "the most pragmatic choice is evident. One daughter is in love, the other seeks revenge. Comingling with Sally, I live—but with Astrid I die. I do not understand this draugar striving for divinity, but if somehow I am the spark, then it is in your interest that I live."

"You're right," he said. "Beyond my daughters' interests, I must do what's best for draugarkind. I've been alive for sixteen hundred years, and in that time, I've learned to doubt the obvious, since I have learned the language of foreknowing and of prophesy. It's probably evident to you comingling with Sally will provide the better odds, and yet I disagree.

"Considering my daughters' histories and proclivities, and with the view of what's at stake for draugar future possibilities, I find it best that you comingle with Astrid. While I respect your right to disagree, there is no time or need for further argument. Tomorrow is Seiðr. I'm sorry, but you have no choice, so you and Sally must comply. Tonight, we drink to Seiðr and to your survival hope!"

October 30 – Seiðr

A song kept going through my head, then gradually, I heard the music and the words.

> *Hey-e-ay, have you ever tried,*
> *Really reaching out for the other side?*
> *I may be climbing on rainbows, but baby here goes:*
> *Dre-e-eams—they're for those who sleep*
> *Li-ai-ai-ai-ife is for us to keep*
> *And if you're wondering what this all is leading to...*

I wanna to make it with you.
I really think that we could make it, girl...

The sound was coming from within my head, from auditory nerve implant, playing in my ears. I did not know, but I was certain it was generated from the power of my thoughts.

"*Are you alone?*" a voice I thought was Sally's spoke above the song.

"*Yes,*" I answered, not yet realizing I responded through my nerve implant.

"*The words you spoke were due to drunkenness, or she was in control of what you thought and said. To my regret, I know that now,*" a saddened Sally said. "*We could have spent a final night in unrestricted love and ecstasy.*"

"*I came for you,*" I strained to say.

"*My father has adjudicated otherwise,*" she answered me. "*For Seiðr, you'll comingle with my sister. You'll comingle with Astrid. She won the legal argument today.*"

"*But it is more than just a legal argument, since Seiðr's purpose is to change the web of destiny,*" I argued then. "*In spite of all that draugar have accomplished, it's obvious you are a dying race. I understand my purpose now. It falls on you and me to alter draugar fate.*"

"*I still believe that draugar destiny will be divinity,*" she said, "*and I am absolutely sure that you will be the spark, but here we are, beset by tragic circumstance: we're lovers, torn apart by fate. Remember now Sidhartha and his call to Earth. When on the verge of destiny, there often is a final and decisive test where character is irrefutably revealed. I'm in my draugar domicile, but I will come to you.*"

Yet even as she spoke, I saw her standing there with French champagne and crystal glasses, wearing only silky lingerie and sexy sandals on her feet. She kissed my lips and led me to the balcony outside my room.

The sun was in the sky, and all along the iron railing, there were twisting vines with brilliant-colored flowers, visited occasionally by butterflies—electric blue, and iridescent hummingbirds, and farther out, I saw a grassy meadow, then a brook, and farther still, a waterfall. A mockingbird had roosted on a branch not far away, and he was singing in an Asian cuckoo's voice.

"You're telling me that we are in a world inside the Earth?" I asked. "It looks as real as any place I've been, and better probably."

"My father and his scientists have recreated paradise, the Garden, symbolizing Enigmatic Choice, and then the Tower, bridging Physical and Spiritual. There's total balance here, and harmony."

"Except that you are killing tens of thousands every year," I said. "You're bringing humans here to die."

"There's no one here who didn't choose to come," she sighed. "Don't kill my buzz."

"It's *enigmatic* choice—the web, as you have said—the moth to flame. They cannot help themselves."

"True, we regret and mourn the human loss, since we respect all forms of life. As recompense, we've cured diseases plaguing human populations, and within this week, we've isolated the genetic factor that we need from living human blood. So after Seiðr, we will close this world to draugar coming in and going out, except for those who choose to seek divinity."

"And all the other draugar—those who choose to live *on* Earth, who have no hope for things divine?"

"The factor and genetic therapy will be available for any draugar wanting it. For those who chose to live above the ground, no longer will they have a need to kill or gather for Seiðr, which like the human Christmas custom and tradition, is derived from pagan ritual, and does not have a spiritual significance."

"And what of us? Of you and me?" I asked. "Will we comingle then for Seiðr in the ritual tonight?"

"It's silly you pretend you don't already know. My father has decided. You'll comingle with Astrid tonight."

"I can't!" I said in protest. "Better yet, I won't. If not with you, I'd rather die unconsummated, uncomingled, unfulfilled."

"*Les jeux sont faits.* The die's already cast," she said. "You were aware Astrid would make a claim for you. You knew that she had legal grounds. Yet undeterred, you came... *because you want to be with her!*"

"Bullshit! *You left me there!* I came because it was the only way to get to you," I answered. "What was I to do? Pretend I never loved or rediscovered life with you? My eyes are open. How can I go back to what I was? I've vowed to love you, Sally, to the end. Yes, I am not deterred, and we have time. What can we do to change this tragic fate?"

"There's nothing we can do. You must comingle with Astrid," she said while sobbing in my arms. "Consider it already done. A fate is cruel that makes a mockery of love!"

I held her close and felt her heart was weeping too, along with mine, which threatened bursting from my chest.

"Your father has no arbitrary power to adjudicate our destiny," I grieved aloud. "Whatever he has reasoned logically is subject to *divine* authority, where love surpasses all. Comingle with me now!"

I kissed her lips and neck and shoulders, trying to convince her, seeking to seduce. I took her to the bed, undressing her, caressing her, and spoke poetic lines that journeyed from Erato's lips to mine.

She weakened while she clasped me close, her fingertips positioned, pressing at my spine and temple, driving me to near delirium. The thought of dying sparked a glimmer of enlightenment, and I was ready to embrace contented death when Sally disengaged and stood.

"I cannot disobey my father's ruling," she lamented. "The dilemma always is the same: choose flesh or disobedience. It's either carnal selfishness or subjection to a higher purpose, which will often hide a mystery. We can't comingle—not like this!"

"When choice itself is disobedience," I then complained, "we'll never move beyond our destiny as ants and spiders crawling on the Earth. If we are helpless to do nothing but obey, then we cannot transcend the physical in order to become divine!"

I tried to hold her there, but she became increasingly intangible while phasing from my room to hers. I watched her weeping eyes as every time she reappeared, her likeness dissipated till she was not there.

"*I cannot do this thing with you, my love, until I know I've found the place and time where you and I belong together. I'm not sure just where and when it is, but when we're there, we'll know. It breaks my heart. Comingle with Astrid and live so we can find that future time and place! Goodbye.*"

Then every trace of her was gone. I could not feel her in my heart or hear her in my head. My sadness was profound, and yet I swore an oath, a boldly-issued challenge, calling out to destiny: *You have no jurisdiction over me, so do your part. There is no greater power than the love within my heart!*

I closed my eyes and saw her face, and in that moment, I defeated death. I would comingle with Astrid, but only so that I might live to strike a blow at fate! The song continued in my head.

> *Li-ai-ife can be short or long,*
> *Lo-a-a-a-ove can be right or wrong,*
> *And if I chose the one I'd like to help me through,*
> *I'd like ta make it with you.*

*****

When I awoke, the sun was gone, but there beyond the balcony were moon and stars. A homesick nightingale from far away intoned the prelude to the Seiðr ritual, and looking out, I saw the tower glowing, felt the agitated energy of life on edge. I heard the sounds of ecstasy, relinquishing control and sighs of silent death while knowing soon Astrid would come for me.

I remembered thinking then that I was always comfortable with Mel, who was divine, and wondered why was I so nervous waiting for Astrid? I felt a physical attraction when I kissed her on the night before, though it was tempered by a healthy fear.

Astrid was cruel and unpredictable, and unlike Sally, didn't value sacred institutions, morals or authority. Estranged from Sally, I felt vulnerable. To calm my feelings of anxiety, I sipped a *sang-champagne* and waited on the terrace, dreading the arrival of Astrid.

"Tonight, you're mine!" a female whispered, still unseen, *"and after we comingle, she will be the last thing on your mind."*

To watch her suddenly materialize before my eyes was mesmerizing, challenging reality. She stood there in the person of a goddess, while in every way personifying *Aset*—Isis to the modern world.

Yet most remarkable—her flawless, oiled skin, once alabaster white, was honey brown. In every other way, however, she was recognizable—another draugar novelty. Her pouting mouth with shapely lips, her chin, her cheekbones and exotic eyes comprised the most intriguing face that I had ever seen.

Beneath her slender neck were toned and sculptured shoulders, posed in arrogance. Her breasts were succulent, as ripe and hanging fruit above her contoured waist and hips. Her thighs and legs were firm and muscular, a welcome resting place. A pair of jewel-encrusted sandals held her pampered feet with painted toes. Her fragrant aura was a warm infusion of vanilla, cinnamon and lavender.

She wore a robe of golden silk, appearing gossamer in artificial light, though disappearing all at once beneath the yellow-gilded moon. Her undergarments shone as liquid gold, transforming as her body moved. Her headdress was a solar disc, suspended in between the Apis horns. The aegis on her chest was made of beads from precious gems, including rubies, diamonds and the rarest sapphire stones.

Another garment on her shoulders was extended to wrists, and when she raised her hands, the golden feathers underneath transformed her arms to wings—a potent symbol of divinity. At once I was confused and felt the urge to bow to her. Instead, I sipped again the blood within the champagne flute. She smiled as she approached.

"You can't escape your destiny," she said. "You're fortunate to have this opportunity—a goddess for comingling! It's been two hundred years since I've been laid. I've tempted men and eaten them, and yet until today, they've all been lacking. None are worthy of my keep. But you have lied to me. You've lied to all of us. You're not an ordinary human male, so I demand you tell me what you are!"

"I did not lie to you," I said. "My mother told me long ago, but I did not remember—not until today. The memory of her riddles, secrets, enigmas and cryptic speech began returning at the moment when I first sipped living human blood two nights ago. Until that time, those memories were locked away."

*****

We sat out on the balcony while gazing at the golden Harvest Moon. The reconditioned draugar air was warm, while from the west, there came a gentle breeze. Another nightingale began an aria.

"Enlighten me," Astrid commanded me, "and tell me what you now remember after tasting living human blood."

"My mother was apparently a draugr, and because I was a male, she shielded me and lied to me about my draugar heritage. I never understood. From early on, she warned me never to partake of blood of any kind. She told me it was sacred and belonged to God, that if I ever ate of it, I'd be a creature wretched in God's eyes. So over time, I developed an aversion at the thought of eating blood and spent my life avoiding it. A nosebleed and the blood that oozed from sinuses would make my stomach queasy till I retched."

"Your father then," Astrid insisted, eyes intense, "Do you remember him?"

"I'm sorry, but I don't," I said, "although my mother, sometimes in her sorrow, mentioned him. She said he once was good, but he was turned to wickedness. When pregnant, she abandoned and concealed herself from him, so he would never know he had a son. I never met him, though when I was twelve, she told me he was dead."

"Your father is not dead," she said. "I believe your father is a draugr, and if I'm right, I know exactly who he is!"

"A draugar male?" I asked. "How can that be? Your sister said there were no fertile draugar males."

"My sister lied," she sighed. "She must have known, and that is why she sought you out. I understand it now! Her research led her to your father, and for forty years, she's searched for you. Your father was a fertile draugar male, so you, his son, may just be fertile too!"

"But I am not a draugr male?"

"Yet probably you are. No draugar DNA is pure. We've mixed with other races, so the threshold is at seventy percent—the minimum requirement for draugar functionality. If you are seventy percent, then you are one of us. If not, you're close."

"I still don't understand," I said.

"Your father's DNA was seventy percent or more, and so depending on your mother's DNA, there is a possibility that you were born a draugar male."

"Impossible!" I sighed. "I'm human! Look at me—I age! And I will die! And Sally said there hasn't been a draugr born for several hundred years!"

"Again, she lied," Astrid declared, "because she never wanted anyone to know. She must believe that you're a fertile draugar male. My sister has deceived us all along."

"But Sally loves me," I repeated to myself.

"She knew that once you drank of living human blood, your latent draugar qualities and instincts would appear. She knew a single sip would activate your dormant draugar genes. My sister timed it perfectly."

I closed my eyes and thought, and deep within, I knew Astrid was right. In all my life, I never felt I was as human as the rest and knew somehow that I was different.

*****

"Today, I won the legal argument," Astrid continued then, "so you belong to me, and after we comingle, then I'll have a precious draugar child, and many more."

"I don't belong to you or anyone," I said. "You cannot win me an argument. If I'm a draugr, then I have the benefit of choice."

"You're wrong," she said. "Since nothing can be proven yet. You don't have legal status—not tonight. You have no choice but to comingle and submit to living blood exchange."

"If I object," I answered her, "then who can make me do this thing?"

"You're at a disadvantage here. My sister gave you our technology, but you are inexperienced and can't make use of it. You'll realize that fifteen seconds is eternity..." she said, and in an instant, we had moved from sitting on the balcony to lying on the bed.

"You teleported me?" I asked, confused, because there was no nausea.

"You saw me sitting next to you," she said, "but I was also fifteen seconds past the normal pace of time. It took me less than seven seconds to convey you to the bed."

"That means that you are here?" I asked, "and also fifteen seconds forward in the same reality?"

"A crucial fifteen seconds that allows me to reshape my personal, immediate reality," she said.

I barely blinked and there I held another champagne flute, refilled and warm with blood.

"So you can fight, but I can take you if I want, against your will if you prefer. That might be fun, *n'est-ce pas*? However, look at me—reach out your hands and touch my perfect body— grope me if you like and do to me what you've imagined doing from time we met. You know you want to squeeze my breasts and ass, you want to rub my legs and thighs, to feel my body close to you, absorbing you. Comingling would be your carnal fantasy fulfilled!"

When next I blinked, my shirt was off, and seeming seconds later, we were naked underneath the sheets.

"I see our destiny," she said while licking from her glass. "We'll let the foolish, idealistic draugar close their gates and slip away to nothingness, since being one with God requires sublimating individuality. But we'll remain on Earth to rule pathetic humans, killing first the males, the wealthy and the arrogant. Together we'll establish an uncompromising draugar sovereignty and propagate our dynasty. To humans, we'll be gods. I'll rule as queen, with cohorts as my princesses and governors, and you my consort, always at my side to honor me."

"Your consort? You're delusional!" I scoffed. "You won't have draugar science or technology, so other than unending life and greater strength, you'll never have the means to subjugate a third-world country, let alone the Earth, since all creation knows that humans have a history of disobedience."

"You underestimate your future mate," Astrid explained. "It's taken many years, but I have managed to convert a number of my father's scientists, so on that fabled day of draugar reckoning, when we are forced to choose, they'll side with me and stay above the ground. These scientists have estimated it will take perhaps one human generation born and buried to create a separate facility with functions to restore technologies for draugar living on the surface of the ground. Then it will be your duty to unite the earthly draugar under me."

"I think you've had too much to drink," I said. "If I am draugar, as you say, or if comingling makes me so, I'll not be ruled by you or anyone."

I tried to stand to leave the bed, but when I looked again, I saw her longing face, as she had sometime—fifteen seconds in the future—straddled me, had pinned me down. It was surreal. I threw her off a second time and stood, but there I was again, beneath her as she pressed a nerve that caused an instant rise, which I was helpless to control.

"I'm taking it!" she said. "You might as well enjoy. I know I will! It's been two hundred years for me!"

I pushed her off again, but she returned aggressively—and this time I was buried in her keep.

"There's no use fighting me," she laughed, "but go ahead, since I enjoy the sport of taking what I want from males!"

Astrid was right to say that fifteen seconds was eternity. She quickly countered every movement that I made, predicted every stunt and thought. She wore me down, and when I thought I'd finally succumb, it seemed I heard a voice.

"*He isn't yours to take, Astrid!*" the voice asserted in the room, "*I cannot let you kill him in your lust for blood! He is already draugar, so comingling will serve no useful purpose in the Seiðr ritual."*

"You dare to interfere, *putain!*" Astrid called out while getting off the bed. *"You dare to interrupt comingling!"* She grasped me by the throat, and flicking out a tiny dagger, strapped against her wrist, she seemed prepared to slash my jugular vein.

"You've violated sacred draugar law! Reveal yourself or he will die!"

When Sally showed herself beside the bed, her purpose was revealed. She held a sword and shield, prepared to fight. She even had a helmet on. Astrid reacted, tossing me aside and teleporting somewhere else, but she returned a minute later ready to engage, with hidden daggers and a trident, armor and a net.

"One web, one spider, to the death!" Astrid declared.

"The end of one of us tonight!" her sister, Sally said, and in an instant, both were gone.

*****

A little more than fifteen seconds after that, the heavy clangs of metal drew me to the balcony, where in the distance, I could see Astrid and Sally in the public square, engaged in mortal competition, struggling hand-to-hand and swinging weapons, striking blows... and even drawing blood.

Without a thought, I grabbed my robe and leapt down thirty feet onto the ground, though even as I rushed toward Sally and Astrid to broker armistice, I found myself within the clutches of another female draugr, seeking to comingle on the spot, but I was snatched away by yet another female with a pretty face and whose exquisite body clung to me, and she was glowing blue. I grasped her wrists and I rejected her, as other draugar suddenly began appearing all around—an audience, at least five hundred strong, and all were naked—none were wearing clothes.

Beleaguered as I waded through the crowd of shapely, firm and flawless naked female figures there, I felt a certain sexual energy and eager hands that groped my body parts, the frantic fingers at my spine.

Intoxicated by the pheromones of human masculinity, their hunger still remained intense, enhanced by earlier comingling, an indication they were in a definite excited state. They offered breasts to me of every shape and size and shade, along with sculptured legs that teased and sought to wrap and capture me. The pleasures offered were excruciating to endure, but I remembered Sally and the hope we shared.

Astrid emerged the better fighter, based on her experience, but Sally had more heart and more intensity. Along with all the draugar in the public square, I watched as Sally fought for me, against apparent overwhelming odds.

We saw her suffer blows and wounds, inflicted by her sister with unnecessary cruelty. We watched as she endured the mockery, humiliation, assassination of her body and her will. The more she weakened, I was more determined to disrupt the *status quo*, but I was helpless standing there against the telling of a story written long ago.

I closed my eyes and pleaded for her life. *"Please help us, Mel!"*

Yet even then, Astrid assaulted Sally with a shield directly to her bloody face, a blow that knocked her sister to the ground and left her dazed. Astrid stood over her, and reaching up, she plunged the dagger into Sally's abdomen and groaned while twisting, burying the blade. As Sally wept, she looked toward me, our eyes locked in a final gaze.

"Please live so we may love again!" she said unto my mind.

Astrid withdrew the blade and raised it to administer *le coup final*, but Erick Draugar suddenly appeared before her murderous resolve was realized, and with a brilliant flash of light, all draugar disappeared, which left me standing all alone within the public square.

Yet only then I realized that I was living fifteen seconds in their past, because they were manipulating time. Whatever I was seeing happened fifteen seconds earlier, which meant the final outcome—whether Sally lived or died—already was resolved.

What's next for me? I thought. With Sally gone, there was no purpose for my being there. Astrid could claim me as her property, but not if I survived comingling. It was my only chance—to live and hope that Sally somehow had survived.

I tried to activate the panel on my wrist to access draugar science and technology. Specifically, I managed to access the wrist control and duplicated sequences that Sally and Astrid had used, and then I focused on returning to a place I'd been.

*****

To my surprise, I phased—I alternated back and forth at first—and then I teleported there, into the tower, where three scientists remained. They balked at first to see my subtle, fading bluish-green, but I convinced them I had come for Seiðr, that I came to alter draugar destiny. They sampled blood and DNA and welcomed me and taught me how to use the interface embedded at my wrist... and shared an ancient draugar prophesy.

They told me fluid time would make my vision blurry, but in time my eyes would compensate. Then after thanking them, I teleported back, returning to my room. I waited, sensing overwhelming static energy within the atmosphere, and so I went out to the balcony and listened, hearing sounds of human male and female draugar ecstasy.

The Seiðr ritual was reaching climax when Astrid returned to claim me as her prize.

"Where's Sally—where's your sister?" I demanded right away.

"One web—one spider. Sally's dead," Astrid proclaimed. "I opened up her chest and ripped from there her throbbing, quickly-beating heart. I squeezed it while astonished, Sally watched me drain her blood from there and drink in celebration of revenge and victory. She's dead and burned. I saw to that!"

"Then legendary draugar immortality is relative?" I asked. "Apparently, it's not impossible to kill a draugr then?"

"A human cannot kill a draugr," she explained, "since humans are inferior in every way, and therefore only draugar have the means and skill to kill a draugr who opposes them."

"And that's why draugar hide from humans deep within the earth?" I asked, "and why superior spiders cannot win in conflicts when opposed by colonies of ants?"

As I approached Astrid, I sensed desire to comingle and a passion that she fought to hide or overcome. I pushed her back against a wall and kissed her bloody lips while wondering if the blood I tasted came from Sally's heart. I pulled Astrid against me and I kissed her neck and shoulders, groping, grasping both her wrists and dragging her into the room, and all the while, I gauged the limits of her corporal strength, determining I could overpower her.

I forced her to the bed and pinned her down, and while restraining her, I wedged my pelvis in between her thighs until I felt the heated fire burning in her keep. She feebly feigned resistance as I tore her blouse and ripped the shreds of purple silk from shoulders, breasts and arms. I thought revenge for Sally when my fingers wrapped around her sister's neck. I squeezed and watched her face and eyes, so vulnerable, as though she trusted me.

I thought to strangle her, to watch her helpless while she died, betrayed by draugar arrogance. Ambivalent, I hated her—and yet, while lying there between her thighs, I wanted to comingle her.

As if she read my mind or was manipulating time, she laughed and wrapped my body with her legs, supple fingers finding neural placements on my spine and face. She arched her back and locked her body onto mine, applying pressure, causing pleasure to delirium. I struggled, seeming paralyzed, and fought to maintain consciousness.

"Why do you fight?" she whispered in my ear, "since destiny cannot be overcome tonight, and you are but a player in a story written long ago by Fate. Initially, you were convinced you loved my sister—that was misdirection meant to lead your listeners astray, and Sally was a minor character who died for purposes of tragedy."

"A story written long ago?" I asked. "By Fate?"

"You know her by another name," she said, "but she's manipulated your entire life, your every word and deed. She even wrote your character to question destiny, to write her stories for a larger audience. She cultivated the illusion of free will and made you think that you could choose, so that volition was indeed your inspiration and your fantasy."

"You're wrong," I mumbled as I strained to free myself from her embrace. "I am the master of my destiny!"

"You're just a feeble ant within my web, whom I will eat!" she laughed. "Relax, enjoy your final destiny!"

I focused on her previous words. She said my story had been written long ago by Fate, and that I knew this writer by another name. I thought about it, wondering if I could believe Astrid, since that would mean I was betrayed by someone dear to me—my Muse, Melpomene.

*****

Alas Melpomene! Why had she chosen me, so young and desperate for wisdom and eternal life? I thought about my work, which all considered, was her gospel for transcending tangibility? And what was her connection to Astrid—though more intriguing, how did Sally factor in? Reflecting on my history, it seemed Melpomene had been there all along, yet I remember her protecting me, rewarding me and guiding me... and even loving me. Astrid had forced me to consider something crucial at the very moment that my scepter slipped into her secret keep: the nature of Melpomene.

For many years, I thought that my imagination made her real and never actually believed that she had power over me, but what if I was wrong? And what if she, a female creature, lacking corporeal identity, was using me to publish her ideas and thoughts? Was I the actual author of the strange, extraordinary stories that I wrote, or was I just a foolish scribe who copied down her words? And worse—was I no more than just a character that she created, meant to demonstrate her unconventional philosophy? A shadow on a darkened screen?

"Melpomene was born of flesh and blood five thousand years ago or more," Astrid replied, unqueued, "and one of nine who have transcended flesh and blood in order to attain divinity. She's mastered understanding on the sub-atomic plane, which means that she is able to manipulate the structure of a universe in which no more than three percent is known or understood.

"She understands the shadowy dark energy abounding even in the human brain, but more than that, her daughter had a child who would fulfill an ancient draugar prophesy—to manifest the spark divine through birth. I am her daughter's daughter, born of destiny, appearing to provide all draugar conscious opportunity to gain divinity. She recognized your purpose on the day that you were born because you have the spark. Tonight, you fertilize the draugar womb as nothing but a drone."

*****

I felt betrayed and angry, so I snapped, and suddenly the webs that bound me fell away. I broke her hold on me, and rolling her onto her back, I pinned her to the bed, my fingers at her throat.

She laughed and tried escape through time manipulation, but I followed her ahead those fifteen seconds of eternity, where I remained on top of her while squeezing at her throat with quivering grasp and covering the panel on her wrist with my free hand.

"Conspiracy!" she screamed as terror filled her eyes. "Who taught you how to slip ahead in time? It's cardinal Draugar law and punishable by death: *no human or unproven draugr may acquire draugar science and technology.* You'll die along with any draugar who instructed you!"

"But you are wrong, Astrid," I said. "Tonight, within the tower, it was proven by your scientists and priests that I am draugar too, which means comingling my blood with yours is now superfluous. I'm legal now. I had no knowledge that was a latent draugar all along and that my draugar DNA was activated when I tasted an initial sip of living human blood. So here I am, a fertile draugar male between your legs... with power over you."

"A fertile draugar male? You know it to be true? So we'll comingle bodies then?" she asked, excited as her fingers found their places.

"Yes, I will get enormous pleasure out of taking you, Astrid," I said, "and watching you submit while on your back, a helpless female as I force my will on you."

"In all my life, I never have submitted to a male, and yet I will endure it, just as long as I will have your seed!"

Our bodies locked in passionate embrace, my fingers hovered in the charged electric field above her skin. I watched her straining face to see where all the secret pleasure places pulsed within and tested them, so I remembered them, and then I arduously repeated that same process with my lips.

Her body was exquisite, from her perfect toes and pretty feet, her slender ankles, shapely legs and sculptured thighs, to womanly, proportioned hips and narrow waist, to firm and ample breasts, well-toned arms and shoulders and a luscious neck and then a splendid face so delicate and intricate and seeming innocent that human males were struck in awe. Imagine what it's like to enter that indescribable abode and then imagine something ten times more!

Astrid was all at once a hungry tiger and a docile lamb, a trickle and a waterfall, the burning sun and icy depths, the hardness of a diamond with the luxury and warmth of eiderdown. I spiraled deep into her universe, defying gravity that clung to me. My cells and molecules and atoms strained the bonds of tangibility, and only then the scepter breached the secret keep again.

If Sally had not trained me to resist and manifest my will, I would have then succumbed and lost all consciousness, consumed, transported to a coma I could not escape. Instead I took, and I persisted there between her thighs. She tried to overcome my hunger, using centuries-old techniques.

She tried to take control, but then I found the places on her spine and frame where she was vulnerable, continuing to take what she surrendered lying there, against her will.

The moment came when her restraints could take no more. The reservoir was tested to its boundaries, inlets rushing, streaming, threatening to burst the dam. She tried to cling to me in order to resist the overwhelming force. Our fingers barely touched, and then she was immediately the helpless victim of a surging, sensual, orgasmic pelvic revolution that consumed her body first, before it paralyzed her soul in sensory overload. So violently, Astrid released the pent-up carnal beast she was within, and then she begged me to reciprocate.

I stopped and pried her hands from me. "You'll never have my seed, Astrid," I said. "I dominated you to prove that I could master you, to reaffirm the female curse recorded in the garden prophesy: *Conception is your sorrow— for, contrary you will be, but he will rule you in the end!*"

"No, no!" she said. "You cannot leave me yet! I need your seed! We must fulfill the prophesy!"

"The prophesy was destiny," I said, "but I have come to reinvent the web, to alter what was destined to occur and weave a separate reality."

"How dare you treat me like a whore!" she screamed while leaping on my chest to claw my neck and face. "You cannot disobey the prophesy! I need to have your seed tonight! You can't deny me what is owed! I now believe you are the *Radical*, were born to change the web of destiny!"

"Enough!" I turned and cast Astrid aside to send her crashing to the floor. "How dare you murder your own sister Sally, whom I loved!"

"Because she broke my heart and she deserved to die!"

I watched Astrid as uncontrite, she wept in rage and anger on the floor. I knelt and grabbed her hair while forcing her to look into my eyes.

"I swear that I will use immortal life to be your nemesis!" I said.

"*I am alive,*" I heard in Sally's weakened voice. "*If you would see me, you must come at once!*"

October 31 – Hugr and Munr

"Our time has come at last," he said while seated on a seeming throne. "Last night, we celebrated Seiðr for the final time, since we have fabricated an elixir isolated from that enigmatic factor found in coursing human blood. We're pleased that no more humans have to die so we may live... and pleased that we can separate ourselves from humankind. The gate between this world and theirs must close, so draugar seeking isolation motivated to pursue omniscient purposes are free to focus on eventual divinity."

"I'm young compared to you," I said. "I do not understand. In your attainment of divinity, you're seeking to become *like* God?"

"Relax your mind, and you will understand intrinsically," he answered me. "Our mission is to know God's purpose, meaning we must leave the use of flesh, which limits knowledge and precludes divinity. The punishment for sin was flesh that dies and snuffs out consciousness, and thus our flesh imprisons us, prohibits our approaching God, since flesh and blood cannot attain divinity. But most importantly, we're writers, all of us."

"And once the gate is closed," I asked, "then how are you transformed? How is it possible to achieve this existential change? Will you rely on celebrated draugar science and technology to achieve divinity?"

"Divinity is consciousness and individuality without the flesh," he answered me, "but foremost also unity with God, and cannot be achieved without a *leap of faith*. Despite rebellion, all the universe is helplessly in unity with God, except for those who consciously resist. The choice is obvious and unmistakable, so on this final day, now you must choose to interfere with human destiny or to fulfill your destined draugar role, which is to spark divinity."

"But how?" I begged, "since I don't know what I'm supposed to do. How could I spark divinity?"

"Not you," he said, "but it will be your seed, that spark— that is *The Way*."

"My seed!" I gasped. "My seed with who? Astrid?"

"Your seed with Sally is *The Way*," he said.

"But Sally's dead. Astrid defeated her. She slit her throat and drank her blood from her own heart. She told me that!"

"Relax, my son," he said, "and find relief that Sally is not dead. Since we are closer to divinity, we live in more than one reality. Astrid came close to snuffing out her consciousness, but we are working to repair the injuries. She must be ready to conceive your seed tonight, so when tomorrow morning comes, it will not matter what you choose. Within the Multiverse, choice is irrelevant. You're much too serious."

*****

At once I was transported to the public square, where many draugar were in panic at the prospect of the Day of Reckoning. When midnight came, the gate would close, and they would be on this side or the other side—in unity with God or forced to testify resistance on the Earth.

Beneath the shadow of decision, many draugar wept while realizing they had chosen to relinquish earthly life and their connection to the world and those they loved. I looked around and watched decisions being made—I saw the coming-ins and going-outs, the sad goodbyes and pleas for unity. I saw such sadness and anxiety, considering eternity at stake, and then Astrid was there.

*****

"The Day of Reckoning has come," she said. "I'm sure my father didn't tell you what would happen on the other side. Since you're a draugr now, it's time you knew the truth."

"Your sister, Sally, is alive," I said. "You lied, and now you speak to me of truth?"

"The cat is dead, while yet it lives. I haven't lied to you. It's just that you don't understand the *thought experiment*, the paradox. It's Hugr and it's Munr too. The time is short for you to choose, because the gate will close tonight.

"My sister and my father will remain to chase idealistic notions of divinity, but I return onto the world you've known and loved for all your life. I've chosen to resist the cosmic resonance for unity, and so my fate is sealed. The central Draugar War regarding soverignty was fought last night, and I have lost.

"Tomorrow I am banished, naked, cast upon the surface of the Earth, without a link to draugar science and technology— no teleport ability, no phasing, temporal manipulation, matter- energy conversion or a link to other draugar minds, but I will drag one-third of all my father's followers along with me, and I will rule the Earth, will punish puny humans for their arrogance!"

"You'd ruin all of Earth and humankind?" I asked.

"It is my purpose and my destiny," she answered me, "unless salvation comes from you, which means that you must choose resistance to the cosmic resonance and live upon the surface of the ground to challenge Destiny and test your faith... *without* my loathsome sister's meddling. We felt a definite connection earlier, our bodies two becoming one, exchanging DNA. My sister will be gone, and you will need a mate."

"I'll seek divinity along with those who choose to stay," I said, "since why would I concern myself with selfish humans crawling on the Earth? They never liked me anyway."

"Because your purpose is to save them from themselves," she said. "If you stay in the Draugar world, you might as well be dead. Divinity is for the venerable and wise—not for a little boy who hasn't lived or gained from lessons of experience. It is a cherished state of death within the memory of God. Your mission is to save the world. I know you feel it in your heart! Your staying in this Draugar world betrays your very destiny."

"And you, Astrid? How could you rule on Earth?" I asked. "Without your father's draugar science and technology, the ants will overwhelm, and if you dare to raise your head, they'll understand the threat you pose. With singular intent, they'll hunt you down, and one-by-one, your once-immortal followers will die. So, while omniscient draugar in this place become divine, rebellious draugar on the surface of the Earth will be destroyed by humankind, to be transformed to human myth and fantasy, to follow in the path of *nosferatu* and *neanderthal*."

"My followers are more than forty-seven-thousand strong, and that includes a dozen scientists who have the knowledge necessary for the duplication of my father's draugar science here, but it will take one human generation, born and dead, before the day of draugar rule will come. Until that time, you'll give me sons, and daughters best of all. We'll propagate a royal order, and we'll constitue a new, eternal pantheon—the greatest gods of earth."

"You're crazy if you think that I would ever be a part of such an egoistic plan," I said. "It goes against my very nature and the efficacy of serving the Almighty God. If I stay here, I'll seek divinity, though now I'm questioning if I am ready for an uninformed eternity. Though if I choose to live upon the Earth, I'm fated to fulfill a role that I am ill-equipped to carry out—to save humanity, which *cannot* be my destiny!"

"You are the *Radical*, you idiot!" she said, "were born to alter destiny, which cannot be with Sally in this place. This 'oneness' that they seek is truly '*death*' in human terms! That should be obvious by now. They've chosen death because they've come to hate their immortality. There is no consciousness beyond this life. There's only peace in death, and comfort in the memory of God."

"My single purpose on the Earth will be to see that you will never rule," I said. "I'm certain I'll convince your followers that you have lost your mind, that forty-seven thousand draugar cannot dominate a human population over seven billion strong. The ratio exceeds one hundred eighty thousand humans for your every draugr on the Earth."

"How many humans truly rule the Earth today?" she asked, supremely confident. "I'm certain you would be surprised, but why not take a guess?"

"One hundred, two hundred maybe," I proposed.

"Yet only fifteen individuals would be a better estimate. The Earth is ruled by fifteen humans from the warlike states of England, China, India, United States and Russia, Israel, Iran, Japan and Germany, Korea—North and South, Saudi Arabia, Brazil and France, and finally the Vatican. When I replace those fifteen humans, I will rule the Earth. Our children will be heads of state and will report to me."

"I'll never give you children. I will pledge my life to foil what you've planned."

"But you don't know what you are up against, when over forty-seven thousand draugar choose to live on Earth, when I will be their potentate. You can't defeat us all. You might as well be part of us. Consider this advantage: you will be the consort of the Queen of Earth. You'll spend your nights at pleasuring the most attractive female creature who has ever lived!"

"I have one human generation, born and dead?" I said, "to save the world, since after that, your followers will reacquire draugar science and technology, and more than biologically immortal, you will be unstoppable. I have until that time to change the destiny of Earth."

"Remember that I am a writer too," she said. "I stand with forty-seven thousand loyal draugar at my side, while you alone are set in opposition to a fate that is inevitable. You'll change your mind and serve the pleasure of your queen," she whispered as she kissed my lips. "The future is a story written long ago..."

I watched her disappear and then I stood alone within the public square, amazed by all I saw. I closed my eyes and thought of being home and seated in my sacred space, and when I opened them, I was at my desk.

*****

"*It's good to have you home,*" I heard in a familiar voice. I felt her seated at my right and watched as Mel appeared. "*You've learned to teleport,*" she said, "*and rest upon the outer edge of time. You've always known that you were not a human male.*"

"It's sad to me," I answered her. "I'll always have a human heart."

"*Your mind will overcome your heart in time, since hearts are flesh and blood, while minds are made of mystic and etheric elements.*"

"You lied to me," I said. "You never told me you were draugar long ago."

"*It is impossible for me to lie,*" she said. "*I've never been a draugr, though their line has come from me. My father's father was divine, my father half-divine. We were children of the Nephilim, and we were called the Eljo, seventeen of us—the only eljo who survived destruction of that wicked ancient world. Unlike the others, we were innocent, and we inclined our hearts and souls toward God, and therefore when the waters came, we were preserved within a lofty mountain crypt, a cave that kept us safe and dry and warm.*

"*Within this crypt, a certain female suffered spider-bite that caused a fever, made her lose her mind and caused her to revert to violent eljo practices. Within one night, she murdered all the males—all eight of them while in their sleep. When morning came, the others found the mangled bodies in a heap, and then they found her resting peacefully, her fever gone. 'Why did you do this awful deed?' they asked. She answered, 'it was Destiny, since I do not remember doing it. Perhaps it was an act of God and purposed to dilute our race.'*"

"No punishment for her?" I asked. "She murdered all the males!"

"*The nine of us who lived would therefore have no equal in a male.*"

"So now I understand! *You* were that girl, Melpomene. You are the Muse of Tragedy!"

"*When Earth was dry again and we could leave the cave,*" she said, ignoring me, "*then we went out and copulated with the sons of men. We were the mothers of the demigods and tribes that ruled the world. The lilu were my daughter's daughters, and the nosferatu, alukahs, vetelas, vrykolakas, strigoi, guaxas, jangshi and the adze were daughters of my sisters by the sons of men.*

"*Those ancient tribes are dead, except the draugar on the Earth today. Eventually, the eljo, nine in number, understood and crossed the river to Divinity. The draugar are the daughters of the goddess Sekhmet of the Siren sisterhood, the daughter who I bore, who is the mother of Astrid, who seeks the spark from you.*"

"But who am I?" I asked. "A month ago, I fancied you a phantom of my overworking mind."

"I chose you long before your father's father's birth because I knew that you would have the spark—that once eternal, you could, over time, become divine."

"A month ago, I thought I was a human male. I struggle to believe a story that belies all comprehension and all thought."

"It is a story written long ago. You have no choice beyond the character I wrote."

"So what am I supposed to do?"

"Your Sally's lost to you. Remain with me. I offer you divinity and everlasting life," she said. *"You are my mate and compliment, the echo to my call for love, the end of loneliness for me.*

"You're right to be suspicious of Astrid, and Sally was a selfish little whore. With me, you'll understand the ecstasy that is divine. Besides, it doesn't matter what you think. You have no choice beyond the role I wrote for you."

"But I'm a writer too, and I imagine something very different," I said.

"That isn't possible," she disagreed. *"You're thinking like a human, when the humans always get it wrong. I've made an offer you cannot refuse."*

"I've grown beyond the feeble role you wrote for me," I said. "I'm not the character you wrote, not anymore, and I'm re-writing as we speak. I'm re-imagining the web, and in my version of the story, I can choose what I will do. I have decided to remain on Earth to save the humans from Astrid, and after I have ruined what she's planned, then I will go to Sally to pursue eternity and perhaps divinity with her."

"How can you be so foolish and disloyal?" Mel in anger sneered. *"I guided you and have protected you from birth. I educated you. Those wicked sisters sought to steal the spark from you! And you would choose that strumpet Sally over me!"*

"You kept the truth from me, manipulated me. You gave me no ability to choose, but Sally risked her life so I would know the truth."

"You cannot know the truth if you don't understand the cosmic language of the universe. Your eyes are ever closed, so what you think you see is nothing more than fantasy. Regain

your senses, husband, take your rightful place beside me as my compliment."

I looked, and in her hands, she held two fruits.

"I've taken from the tree of knowledge, so that you could learn the cosmic language of the universe, but I have also taken from the tree of life, so you will be divine. So eat, and let us live as gods!"

"I am no god," I said, "and I don't wish to be a god. My purpose is to save humanity. I have the opportunity to save them from Astrid, and that is what I choose to do."

"You cannot change a story written long ago by me."

"Of course I can and will. I am the *Radical*, which means that I was born to alter destiny."

"You'll try, but you will fail," she said, *"and then you will return to me, though maybe I will not receive you favorably—not after your disloyalty to me and time has passed. Perhaps I'll find another male to take your place."* She dropped her robe, exposing all at once her nakedness. *"But eat and you will understand. Come, husband, to your wife."*

And only then I realized how much Astrid resembled Mel in beauty and in arrogance, but Mel possessed divinity. I didn't dare to look at her directly, fearing I would lose possession of my mind and will, and yet her naked body caused such wanting in my heart that I succumbed and looked upon surreal perfection in the female form.

My fellow brother males—I swear I wanted to resist the script she wrote, but I was helpless. I was hypnotized, a struggling insect in her sticky web.

I fell onto my hands and knees, and straining, crawled to her and kissed her feet of flesh, so soft and warm and perfect to my eyes. I slowly rose, while kissing first her ankles, legs and knees, succumbing to her will, succumbing to the script she wrote, and yet before I touched or tasted of the fruit, a second female intervened.

I recognized her face, since when I was a younger man, she sometimes sat and wrote through me. I knew her as the Muse of Comedy. Her name was Thalia, beautiful and equally-divine, a counterbalance to Melpomene. She took my arm, commanding me to stand, and took a place between myself and Mel.

"*Inanna,*[25] *sister of eternity,*" then Thalia said, "*I intervene tonight because I have no choice. He is the Radical, and so his destiny is not with you. When we were seventeen, you slaughtered all the males, and so your curse is loneliness in perpetuity, for Fate will never have it otherwise, and Destiny proclaims that you will never hear an echo to your call for love.*"

"*Asima,*[26] *cruelest cousin,*" Mel returned. "*I chose this male and nurtured him. I plucked a coarse, unpolished pearl from countless pebbles of the shore, and I alone have found the spark of light in him. I gave him sight to pierce the veil of tangibility and rudimentary understanding of the cosmic language that we speak.*

"*He understands what you have said. See how his eyes protest! See how he loves and worships me! How could you take my well-earned prize when you have known that I have been alone, unloved since from the day we left the cave. Perhaps you want him for yourself?*"

"*His staff is meant for Sally's womb tonight, but neither will she have him as her echo,*" Thalia said. "*His destiny is with Astrid, your daughter's daughter, who will seek to rule the world of blood and flesh. Their fates are intertwined for good and bad, an answer to the cosmic riddle written at the start of measured time and history.*"

She turned to me. "*I know that you have loved Melpomene, and she loves you. Look one more time upon her face, as that will be your last.*"

I turned, and when I looked upon Melpomene a final time, I saw such loneliness and sorrow in her heart, and I imagined her existence, felt it as she kissed my lips and whispered in my ear. To live eternally alone, unloved, untouched—that was her punishment for slaughtering the eljo males.

---

[25] *Inanna* – the ancient Sumerian goddess of love, beauty, sex, desire, fertility, war, combat, justice, and political power.

[26] *Asima* – the West Semitic goddess of Fate, sometimes depicted as the personification of Fate.

I saw regret and pain profound in her despondent eyes before they melted into tears, and then I saw an upturned mouth that howled and frowned before she hid her weeping face and disappeared. I bowed my head and wept for her, her melancholy aspect burning in my brain, the very memory and face of Tragedy.

"*She's such a drama queen!*" a smiling Thalia laughed, "*a victim of her spleen. The gate between the worlds will close in seven hours' time, so you must go to Sally for a boffing that's sublime. She waits, and she is ready for your glow within her secret keep! Go sow your seed and let it grow, and Fate will plant what Earth will reap!*"

*****

I felt the ridges of her fingertips as soft they trailed along my face, caressed vermillion lines on Cupid's bow and rested at my temples, thumbs beneath my chin to frame my face. Then leaning close, she lightly touched my lips with hers, and after teasing, then she pressed and kissed my mouth. Her tongue began a delicate and tender *pas-de-deux* with my own tongue to stimulate arousal, reaching from my groin to all extremities— and even to the tiny hairs that covered me and stood on end.

"I thought that you were dead," I said.

"We live in more than one reality, a Multiverse" she answered me. "This Multiverse is full of those who write, but Destiny will write the Master Script, so all the story lines must be rewritten as mere radials that are supporting structure for her Master Web of Fate, extending to the outer reaches of all time and space. The egocentric story that my sister told you was rejected for a better-drafted, comprehensive, thought-provoking script my father wrote. In his I am alive, as you can see."

"So in your father's version then," I asked, "what happens next? He is your father, after all. If he's the author of my role tonight, he knows exactly what I want to do to you... and he's okay with that?"

"He also knows what I have planned to do to you, although I'm sure it makes my father blush."

"And after our comingling is done? Then I return to live upon the surface of the Earth? The gate is closed, and you are lost to me?"

"We'll have eternity," she said, "where nothing lost is ever really lost. In time, our paths will cross again, and if we have succeeded at our trials and learned from them, we'll understand those things that vex us as we say goodbye tonight. We cannot let uncertainty of what will come control our living days and hours, minutes, seconds as they will arrive. Each day is like another lifetime lived, each morning a unique and single opportunity."

She kissed my lips again.

"The draugar who have chosen to exist on Earth will have the benefit of life eternal, never needing human blood, as they will have the factor in a supplement, but they will lose the benefit of draugar science and technology—no teleporting, time manipulation or the link to other draugar minds. So you, alone, will have those capabilities, but you will need those gifts and more, considering the odds of one to stand against an army forty-seven thousand strong. I've read the script, though I cannot reveal the plot to you, and yet I know that you will win, because you are indeed the Radical."

"So have you have read the story that your father wrote?" I asked. "What of Astrid?"

"Eventually, Astrid will be your wife," she answered me, "and mother to your sons and daughters born."

"No, no!" I said with anger and determination in my voice. "Your father wrote it wrong! Astrid will never be my wife and mother of my children born!"

"I see it in your eyes," she said, "I sense that you already know. You've known it from the moment that you met her in that San Francisco karaoke bar. She's irresistible to you."

"She isn't irresistible to me. You are the only female who I love. I'll never love another after you. I'll mute my heart until again it beats in harmony with yours. I'll write a story better than your father did. Melpomene has taught me well."

"Do you forget, my love? Melpomene—the spider-bitten, is the Muse of Tragedy," she sighed. "You'll understand all things in time, but we have something better to accomplish now, which is comingling our blood and flesh."

*****

We kissed again, this time abandoning restraint. Our clothes were cast aside, our bodies all at once entwined while finding finger frets in pleasure places on each other's forms. Our lips and tongues explored the nether reaches of erotic possibility. The scepter and the secret keep were rendered bare and vulnerable by our arousal, growing warm and wet, engorged, anticipating consummation of our love.

The chamber held a soft and cushy bed with satin sheets, both red and white, the petals of one thousand roses scattered all about—their scent a strong *parfum*. Beside the bed there was a strange machine with shiny metal cuffs, with blinking lights and hoses running to a reservoir, and on a stand, two flutes of *sang-champagne*. I recognized the music as the second movement, called *Romanze*, by Mozart, thirteenth Serenade.

I felt as though my every vein and artery would burst as Sally slid her body onto mine, and every time she rose and fell, I thought my heart, which pounded even in my ears, was ready to explode within my chest. Yet only then, I understood the spider male, and why he risked such jeopardy.

If I had died right then, with Sally's womb embracing me, it would have been a blissful death, demise in perfect ecstasy. I clung to consciousness as Sally trapped me in her silken keep, and looking down, she smiled at me.

"I said I like to be on top," she purred, "but worry not. When I have had my fill, then you may have me as you like."

For several hours we remained entangled, sometimes gentle, voicing sighs and moans, while sometimes powerful and loud, with thrusts that shook the bed and rocked the room. With every time I reached my zenith and I fell, her rise and fall came closer to my own until we rose and fell in flawless synchrony. I gave her everything I had and lay, exhausted, next to her, my muscles twitching, though unable to respond.

She straddled me and clamped my shoulder with one shiny cuff, and when she locked it on, I felt a piercing right below my clavicle. She smiled and clamped the other onto her and cringed as she was pierced. Then after stretching out her naked body on my own, she activated the machine. She kissed my mouth and wrapped me in a spiderlike embrace.

"And now our blood will drain into the separate reservoirs, three liters at the most, a Class IV hemorrhage, which brings about a hypovolemic shock. We'll hover in a place near death for minutes, seeming hours, even days. Our spirits will depart, and yet our minds will bring them back. And finally, your blood will come to me, and mine to you, comingled for all time."

*****

I felt my lifeforce leaving me. My head was spinning, and my heart was racing, trying to compensate for oxygen to my extremities. I felt a tightening within my veins and sudden coldness in my hands, my feet and face. I heaved to breathe, and then I felt a profound calmness passing over me, and opening my eyes, I looked on Sally's face.

Her skin was deathly-white, and yet her eyes were open, never blinking, fixed, her pupils dilated. She did not seem to be alive. I sensed no soul beyond those eyes. Perhaps her injuries when fighting with Astrid had been too much to bear. *To think that thirty minutes earlier, we loved so intimate and passionate. La petite mort!*

It came on suddenly. As I began to feel the warmth of Sally's blood infused into my arteries, I sensed a tingling that permeated every cell. It was a radiance that grew, a body "high" I never had experienced before.

I reveled in the glow, which I cannot describe, except to say I felt a long, enduring orgasm in every molecule in me that lingered, growing, and eventually became too much for my exhausted mind to bear. I lost all consciousness, and yet although my spirit did depart, my sheer determination willed it back. *La petite mort.*

*****

When I awoke, I found myself within my bed in my apartment home on Earth, and on the stand, beside the bed, was Sally's runic ring. I held it in my palm and made a fist, remembering comingling. Was Sally really dead? Was all for naught? I never will forget that look of death I saw upon her face. If Munr caused her spirit to return, I did not see it, not before my spirit and my body did depart.

But now, I was alone upon the earth, and somewhere out there was Astrid, and forty-seven thousand more. The gate between the human and the draugar worlds was closed, and humans had no clue what they were up against. Somehow, I found myself resenting humans as I sat, considering the arrogance of ants. They did not know how small and vulnerable they were as individuals. Collectively, their genius was divine, and yet each human was irrelevant in actuality.

I found my way into my sacred space and hoped to feel Melpomene, but she was gone. No trace of her remained. Remembering my precious Sally's words, I sensed eternity, *where nothing lost is ever really lost*. Melpomene was always writing, spinning silk and weaving webs. Somehow, our paths would cross again, and I'd return the echo in appreciation. I knew that someday I would change her destiny.

While looking toward the clock and then my calendar, I laughed derisively and just that moment realized that "time" would soon become irrelevant to me. With immortality, what need had I for seconds, minutes, hours or days? The idea of an "hour" was absurd, immesurable in context of eternity.

I walked outside and took a place beneath the sun, but all the world seemed different, a darker place. The sky was shadowed in a haze. I saw the stars and moon in darkened light of day. Was this the consequence and price of immortality? To never see the sun again for all eternity? Disheartened, I arrived at Sally's house and found no trace or her, as even Mama cat was gone.

The Golden Buddha seemed to glow unnaturally beneath the altered sun, and in that moment, I remembered Sally's keen interpretation of the statue cast within the moment she was born. It was my *Calling of the Earth to Witness* and my moment of enlightenment. Melpomene and then Astrid had tempted me and threatened me, and yet within that chamber of comingling, when all seemed lost, I overcame my fear and called the Earth itself to strengthen me, so I would live, and thus the Buddha saved my life that day.

"*I bear you witness!*" seemed to roar the very ground on which I sat beneath symbolic *Bodhi* tree.

So there I was, alone upon the Earth. The human ants would swarm me if they know why I was there, and yet the forty-seven thousand draugar on the Earth would bend my will in service to Astrid. While looking out, I saw a female walk toward me, and then another, and another still, and counting, there were several dozen coming after me. I was uncertain what to do. I had the time advantage, so I slipped ahead for fifteen seconds and I teleported to a place outside the coffee shop.

*****

Inside, I looked around, and I could not believe my eyes! It was impossible! There, at my favorite table, at the place that held my dearest memories... was Sally, sitting there. She looked toward me and smiled and summoned me as only Sally would. Entranced, I walked to her and saw that she was eating dirt.

"I thought that you were dead. The Draugar Gate is closed. How is it that you're here?"

"When our comingling was done," she said, "I changed my mind and followed after you. I could not leave you all alone on Earth to battle with Astrid and those who follow her."

"What should we do?" I asked. "I'm here because the forces of Astrid are coming after me."

"Well, first of all, we are the only ones with access to our draugar science and technology. We'll have to modify the implants on our wrists. I'll have to program yours to work in synch with mine, since I know better how to access new technologies beyond the Gate."

She held a shiny instrument that was a cylinder, which flashed an alternately green and amber light.

"It'll only take a moment, but I'll need to see your wrist."

My heart was pounding. I was still in shock to see her sitting there. Could it be real? Had Sally really followed me? Could we have everlasting life and love together on the Earth? And while we'd have to battle forces of Astrid to save the world, at least we'd be together doing it. Yet just before surrendering my wrist, I hesitated, sensing something odd and out of place. *Her hands were different!*

"What's wrong, my love?" she said and kissed my mouth. "We'll be together for all time!"

I strained to slip ahead in time for fifteen seconds and returned, incredulous, though well-informed, and so I pushed away from her and stood.

"I saw it! You are here to wipe the implant on my wrist! You're here to spoil my advantage, to delete my link to draugar science and technology. You look like Sally, but you're someone else! I see it now."

"I'm Sally, darling," she insisted. "Please, sit down. You're new at fluid time, so inexperienced and uninitiated, you're mistaking what you see."

"I saw you wipe the implant! That I know! You're here to take away my sole advantage on the Earth... and now I see Astrid... she comes!" I glanced and watched her walking through the door. I turned back to the Sally counterfeit and sighed before I stood.

"You look like Sally, feel like Sally, taste like Sally, yet I sense you're someone else. Who are you? Tell me now!"

"So close!" she laughed, "and only thirty minutes in! *So easily distracted is the hybrid male!* You stand no chance against our queen, Astrid. A singularity against a single ant! The Gate is closed to you and draugarkind, which means she is the queen to all who now remain on Earth. It's futile to resist, you little fool."

"I'm more than that. I'll tell the humans who you are!"

"Run out and tell the world the truth of your discovery," she mocked, "and see if anyone believes your draugar fantasy. Our queen has come! Accept your destiny."

Astrid first kissed the Sally look-alike and sat, supremely confident.

"So now you see how gullible and vulnerable you are, my little boy," she said. "I'm disappointed actually, since I expected more from you, the so-called *Radical*. I thought that I'd enjoy the challenge and the sport of chasing you, of taming you. Oh well, you must do better than today to prove your worthiness."

"Who is this devious impersonator next to me?" I asked. "Who is this cunning fraud?"

"My future husband, please meet Sally's *cousin*, Marianne, identical in every feature, though undoubtedly more fun than goody-two-shoes-Sally ever was. But you can call her Sally if you want, and she will do for you what Sally never would."

"She'll never be, and you could never be to me what Sally was!" I answered her.

"Lest you forget why you are here," Astrid continued then, "you'll be my husband and the father of our children yet unborn. You'll run, but you will not escape. There is no bad or good—my goal is Motherhood. It's written prophesy. You are the Radical, the fated echo to your destined Queen who called."

I did not notice when I entered, then I realized that every person in the coffee shop was draugar, all prepared to do the bidding of Astrid. At once, the table was surrounded by the female horde, so anxious, slowly closing in.

"I swear to be you nemesis, Astrid!" I answered, fuming and defiant as she smiled so cynically at me. "My purpose is to save the Earth from you, which means I'll write a prophesy anew. I challenge fickeled Destiny to regulate my fate, since I was born the Radical to set all matters straight."

Astrid leaned close and kissed my lips while signaling her followers, yet just before they seized my limbs to wipe the implant at my wrist, I teleported to another place, which for the present, must remain unknown. I need your help.

Adiuva me. Octobris X quid accidit? Masculini sexus, necesse nunc mutant. Veniam autem ad vos per somnium.

www.ingramcontent.com/pod-product-compliance
Lightning Source LLC
Chambersburg PA
CBHW032110280326
41933CB00009B/779